Finding the Abundant Life

Michele Michaels

Foreword by
Erin Thiele

RestoreMinistries.net

NarrowRoad Publishing House

Finding the Abundant Life
Michele Michaels

Published by:
NarrowRoad Publishing House
POB 830
Ozark, MO 65721 U.S.A.

The materials from Restore Ministries were written for the sole purpose of encouraging women. For more information, visit us at:

EncouragingWomen.org
RestoreMinistries.net

Permission from the author has been given to those who wish to print or photocopy this book for themselves or others, strictly for encouragement and informational purposes; however, such copies or reprints cannot be sold in any form without prior written permission from the author.

Unless otherwise indicated, most Scripture verses are taken from the *New American Standard Bible* (NASB). Scripture quotations marked KJV are taken from the *King James Version* of the Bible, and Scripture quotations marked NIV are taken from the *New International Version*. Our ministry is not partial to any particular version of the Bible but **love** them all so that we are able to help every woman in any denomination who needs encouragement and who has a desire to gain greater intimacy with her Savior.

Cover Design by Dallas and Tara Thiele

First Printing: 2007
Second Printing: 2016 Revised
Third Printing: 2019 Revised

ISBN: 1-931800-14-6
ISBN13: 978-1-931800-14-3
Library of Congress Control Number: 2007920996

Table of Contents

Foreword

It's been years since the Feminist Movement robbed women out of their rightful roles and blessings of how God designed women to be. Though it's goal was to give women the same rights as men, it has served to cause women to have no choice but to become single mothers, provide not only for themselves but often their male cohabitant. Women have not freed themselves from men, as it said it was set out to accomplish, but instead, women have become obsessed with having a man, any man at any cost. Not surprisingly the Bible's prophet said times like this would come. Isaiah 4:1 The Message (MSG) says, "That will be the day when seven women will gang up on one man, saying, 'We'll take care of ourselves, get our own food and clothes. Just give us a child. Make us pregnant so we'll have something to live for!"

It's women like *Michele who have been called to blaze the trails for women who will soon find themselves, alone, without a husband or children or family. In this five book series, Michele takes us along on her journey that didn't lead to her regaining what she lost, but finding a relationship so strong, so fulfilling and so peaceful that she is an inspiration to all of us.

Much of what I read in this book, when it was first only available to women in her church, I've used to help the women in my own ministry. Each of us needs to glean the unspoken truths, wisdom and freedom that Michele has experienced and has shared with us in this dynamic book for women.

I'm honored to call Michele my friend, and it's through what she has transparently shared with us in this book that will help us each discover how we can rise above every situation He calls us to go through.

Erin Thiele
Restore Ministries International

Chapter 1

What is the Abundant Life?

The thief comes only to steal and kill and destroy;
I came that they may have **life,** and have it **abundantly.**
—John 10:10

What is the Abundant Life?

The abundant life is the life that I am finally living. It is a life that is "joy unspeakable" because it is full of God's glory! It is a life that, I believe, Jesus died to give us, but very few ever reach in their lifetime! In the Amplified Bible, it defines this life as "abundantly [attaining yet greater perfection in living this life]."

Over the last few months, the Lord has brought me into a new life, a life of abundance. This life seemed something that was unattainable for me and for most Christians. My life was a life of struggle, not a life of ease that Jesus spoke about in Matthew 11:29. "Take My yoke upon you and learn from Me, for I am gentle and humble in heart, and you will find *rest* **for your souls.**"

Though my journey toward the abundant life is not at all complete, I can tell you that I have attained the *rest* for my soul and joy unspeakable, full of glory!!!

"That the trial of your faith, being much more precious than of gold that perisheth, though it be tried with fire, might be found unto praise and honour and glory at the appearing of Jesus Christ: Whom having

*not seen, ye love; in whom, though now ye see him not, yet believing, ye rejoice **with joy unspeakable and full of glory**: Receiving the end of your faith, even the salvation of your souls" (1 Peter 1:7-9, KJV).*

We read verses like John 16:33. *"These things I have spoken to you, so that in Me you may have peace, In the **world** you have tribulation, but take courage; I have **overcome the world.**"* All we ever focus on is *"**in the world you have tribulation,**"* since that is how we live day in and day out.

This life of tribulation, of struggle, of pain and of sorrow is not God's plan. It is not why Jesus came to this world to live and die for us. I believe that we are to live a life of joy that is so incredible you can hardly describe it—a **joy** that is *unspeakable* because it is full of God's glory!!

Just as Jesus' power came through the cross, I believe that it is in our cross that we, too, will attain the power to live this kind of life that is to be envied by the world. Our lives are to be a life that will illuminate the darkness in today's world; a life that becomes a beacon of light to guide the lives of women who are lost in darkness. In the midst of their darkness, our light can point the way to the One who can give them their own abundant life. *"For whatever is born of God **overcomes the world**; and this is the victory that has **overcome** the **world**—our faith" (1 John 5:4).*

May you never forget that *"You are from God, little children, and have overcome them; because greater is He who is in you than he who is in the world" (1 John 4:4).*

Must we wait until we get to heaven before *"He will wipe away every tear from their eyes; and there will no longer be any death; there will no longer be any mourning, or crying, or pain; the first things have passed away" (Rev. 21:4)?*

I used to think so, but not any longer.

Since finding this life, I have had the insatiable urge to share this life with every woman I know! It is beyond freedom, it is far beyond finding peace—it is a life that makes you want to burst out in song and dance!!

This life was not attained through any means that is unavailable or unattainable to anyone. That means that what I have now, you can have, and you can give it to your friends, your daughter, your mother or your sister! Surprisingly, it is not in what I attained, but was, in fact, when I lost everything!

Didn't Jesus tell us that? Were we not listening, or did we not have the right ear to hear it? *"For whoever wishes to save his life will lose it; but whoever loses his life for My sake will find it" (Matt. 16:25).*

As Christians, it seems that we often have a "head knowledge" of this principle and many other principles that Jesus told us about when He ministered to His apostles or when He shared the Beatitudes to thousands—but we don't live that life. We don't walk it out. We have the faith to *believe* that it works, but we don't walk out that faith; therefore, "faith without our works is dead" (James 2:26).

For most of us, our existence is a life that is dead or dying. Yet, Jesus died so that we could have LIFE and have it abundantly! That word *abundantly* means to me a life that overflows with good things—beginning with joy!

Ladies, this life is attainable to each and every one of us. I have found over the course of these past few months that it is found in losing the life that we all struggle to keep. It is in truly surrendering our lives and living out the principles that are all found in the Bible, but are never really lived, that bring that joy that eludes most of us.

In the course of my first restoration, I walked out the principles found in the *Restore Your Marriage* book and attained a restored marriage. However, I walked these principles out with so much fear and trepidation because of the level of my faith at the time. What was worse, however, was that I was seeking the life that I wanted. It never occurred to me that I could be happy (let alone joyful) if God did not restore my marriage. So I prayed specifically (as we are taught in Bible studies to do) and followed the principles (that our ministry has always encouraged a woman to do). Since finding my abundant life (when I lost everything), I realized that Jesus also told us how we were to pray, which was "Thy will be done."

What got my attention was when I began to see the women whose marriages were restored, but were living lives of struggles, pain and heartache, and that motivated me to move from where I had settled in—this side of the Jordan. This side of the Jordan is just next to the desert but sits on the banks of the river. It appears green with abundant water, but it is not the land promised.

Because of the questions sent to me from restored women which were mingled with struggles, pain, fear and bewilderment that I also was experiencing, I set out once again to seek God for what He wanted to do in my life:

"For thus says the LORD of hosts, 'Once more in a little while, I am going to shake the heavens and the earth, the sea also and the dry land . . . The latter glory of this house will be greater than the former,' says the LORD of hosts, 'and in this place I will give peace,' declares the LORD of hosts" (Hag. 2:6, 9).

Honestly, I had no idea what I was searching for, but God was calling me to come higher and to again set off for new and unchartered territory in order to bless His daughters who He had entrusted to me.

What I found was the fountain of youth, the inner peace, the true meaning of life, the secret of life and why we were created—all in an instance. I found it in this verse below that the Lord had given me more than ten years ago but has baffled and confounded me until just weeks ago. I read it almost every day and even spoke to others about what they thought it really meant. I knew God had given it to me, and it just may be the key to unlock the mystery of the abundant life I was searching for.

*"Therefore, thus says the LORD, 'If you return, then I will restore you—Before Me you will stand; And if you extract the **precious from the worthless,** You will become My spokesman. They for their part may turn to you, But as for you, you must not turn to them" (Jer. 15:19).*

It may seem simple enough, but its true meaning had eluded me for years. I reread it, added parts to help it make more sense and even wrote two words to the end of the verse when I asked God to give me more understanding. Here is what I would read "Therefore, [Michele], thus says the LORD, 'If you return, then I will restore you—Before Me you will stand [alone]; And if you extract the precious from the worthless, You will become My spokes[wo]man. They for their part may turn to you, but as for you, you must not turn to them [for hope or help]" (Jer. 15:19).

It was the **"precious from the worthless"** that had me the most baffled. I kept looking at different things in my life and tried to compare them to see if it was *precious or worthless* to sort out if I should *extract* it from my life. It took me so many years to discover what I really knew in my head, but I had to discover it in my heart. Ladies . . .

He is precious—everything else is worthless!

You may think that you know that and think I must be incredibly stupid. However, unless you are living a life that shouts that principle, it is just head knowledge!

I knew that once I "got it" God would call me to be His spokesperson! Prior to this revelation, I was a woman who was happy if she never left her home—now I am traveling around the world! It is this principle, I believe, that changed Jesus' apostles from hiding in an upper room to being men who would be martyred and even hung on a cross.

The abundant life is one that is surrendered. Surrendered to all the wants that we think will make us happy and all the control that we think we need to have on our lives (and the lives of all the people around us). I, like you, thought that this was the life that I was living. I had made Jesus Lord of my life, but I never really contemplated finding the life that I was created for, which I am now finally living.

The first reason we are all created is to fellowship with God. When I began to yearn deep in my soul to walk with God in the "cool of the day" like Adam did, walk with God like Enoch did and see Him face to face as Moses did, I had no idea how to do it. So I asked God to show me how, since all wisdom is from above and He will give wisdom to anyone who asks.

In my search, my heart began to change toward what was motivating me to find out how to have this type of intimacy with the Lord. Instead of wanting it for what intimacy would do for *me,* I found that I soon wanted deep intimacy for Him, my Beloved. I wanted above all to be the woman He created me to be—His companion! I wanted to be so close that we could fellowship together and be as deeply in love with Him (because He deserved that) as He was with me.

The discovery of precious and worthless was found when a missionary visited our church and told a story of a little girl that he had found who was living on the streets and dying. The missionary was called to leave India to come to the states. He had to say goodbye to this little girl, and he knew would it would be the last time he would see her alive. When he hugged her, he was so broken and sad when she said, "You do not need to be sad for me, because I have Jesus. Jesus is all I need. He is everything. I have everything that I need." This year was the second time I had heard the story, but this time it changed my life forever!

I began to tell the Lord that He was all I wanted, He was all that I needed and that if I had Him I had everything I needed! The more I said it, the more He became the love of my life. What I was speaking became what was in my heart! When troubles came against me, I would tell the Lord that He was all I wanted and all I needed. Immediately, whatever came against me no longer mattered, and it lost its sting and its affect over me.

This mindset changed my heart to be able to not just endure, but more than overcome the destruction that came against me (our family and my ministry) with my husband announcing he was divorcing me. It is in the midst of these kinds of crises that you will be brought to heights of joy that become unspeakable!

You will have Him as this little dying girl had Him and how I have Him now. If that were not joy enough, "and all these things will be added unto you," the little girl that was dying was healed, whole and healthy when the missionary returned. She had Jesus, and He was all she needed to live. I am not dying, though my husband just divorced me a month ago, and I am now the single mother of six. But I, too, have Jesus and He is all that I need to live the abundant life!

I hope that this first chapter has increased your thirst and desire to have more of Jesus—to know Him intimately as He becomes everything you want and need. You do not need to let go of anything but simply do what God led me to do. Begin right now to tell Jesus that He is all you want, He is all you need and if you have Him you have everything. When trials come against you say these words over and over again until what is happening (or what has happened) no longer matters.

Say these words when you wake up every morning and when you lay your head down on your pillow at night. Say them out loud, in your heart and when you go into your prayer closet.

When your head knowledge becomes a heart condition nothing will hurt, nothing will bring you to fall apart, and nothing will shake you. If you are hurting, if you are falling apart, if you are shaken or trembling then you need **more of Him.** Precious one, more of Him is not found in reading *about* Him in your Bible, quoting Scriptures or rebuking the devil. It is found in intimacy *with* Him.

That does not mean you no longer read your Bible (these are your love letters and your promises from Him.), and it does not mean that you do not quote Scriptures (since these renew your mind so you think like Jesus does), nor does it mean you no longer pray (just begin to pray by sharing your heart and hurts but leaving what should be done to Him—*Thy* will be done!). As far as the kind of praying that I used to do (the spiritual warfare kind), I have discovered that with the Lord as my Husband He loves to fight my battles for me. My position is by His side, as His bride, to focus on my love and cherish Him as He longs to be cherished.

If you are a wife forsaken and grieved in spirit and a wife who has been rejected, Jesus is calling you to become His bride! Will you?

Will you leave it all behind (the worries, the pain, the questions and the burdensome relationships) and pursue Him alone?

*"For the LORD has called you, Like a wife **forsaken** and **grieved** in spirit, Even like a wife of one's youth when she is rejected,' Says your God... For **your Husband** is your Maker, Whose name is the LORD of hosts; and your **Redeemer** is the Holy One of Israel, Who is called the God of all the earth'" (Isaiah 54:6–5).*

Chapter 2

Finding Your Life

He who has found his life will lose it,
and he who has lost his life **for My sake** will find it.
—Matthew 10:39

During the past few weeks, especially while driving, I have been drawn to a song that my boys sing in their worship band. I enjoy the upbeat nature of the tune, but it is the words that have captivated me.

The chorus says:

"To find your life,
You've got to lose it,
All the losers get a crown."

Less than five months ago, I lost the life that I had lived and actively pursued for 14 years. All my life, I wanted just a simple life of being a wife and mother; I loved, simply loved staying home and not venturing outside my world.

Less than five months ago I was the wife of a pastor of a megachurch and had began a huge women's ministry of thousands, which was founded on my own marriage restoration. I was well-known, admired and loved as a co-pastor (women's pastor of our church), and was often ministering side-by-side with my husband. Even my children held many leadership positions within our church. And due to the media attention our church was given, our family was well known through our area and even statewide.

Our family was clearly high-profile, both here in the United States, and even in many nations. Then, one day, my world as I knew it fell completely—my husband walked into our bedroom and told me that he was leaving that morning for an appointment with an attorney to file for divorce and that his intention was to find another woman to marry.

What do you do when your world falls?

The song that I love to sing says, "And even if my world falls I will say . . . Above ALL I live for your glory!!"

Not immediately, but sometime later, I understood that God had been preparing me for that moment in my life for well over a year. And that meant I was determined to do just that—to live for His glory. I knew that God was in complete control and that no matter what happened, the Lord was all that I needed, and He was all that I wanted. Through my love and trust in Him, I knew, my world falling would be used to give glory to God.

The day the Lord chose to prepare me for my journey was when I heard the sermon I spoke about in chapter 1, or it just may have been a couple of songs I couldn't stop listening to that made me re-examine my life. One spoke of finding my place in this world and was about a person who had once moved mountains, but now was a missing person. I wanted to feel like that again, be the person who felt so alive, able to believe God for the impossible, and live on a limb where only my faith was holding me up.

The feeling ached within me. I had no earthly idea how to get back there, so I often spoke to the Lord each morning long before the sun came up and pleaded with Him, urging Him, to help me to get to that place with Him again.

When I first started my journey at the very beginning when I found RMI and I wanted a restored marriage, it really was more for what it would do for me. It's always where we begin our journeys—when we have a crisis hit our lives. Back then I wanted the pain gone and the shame (of separation and later divorce) removed from my life. And I also wanted a father for my children, and I did not want to be a single parent.

Yet, somewhere during my first journey my focus changed, and with it, my heart changed too. My desire became more of wanting my Lord than a restored marriage. And not surprisingly, as soon as I no longer cared about my marriage being restored, nor getting my husband back, God turned my husband's heart back to me (and toward home), and my marriage was restored.

This change in my focus (and later in my heart) is what happened this time too. I went into this journey for what a closer walk with the Lord would do *for* me. I wanted to feel loved, secure and cherished— simply to feel all the things that every woman wants to feel but can never get from an earthly husband. Soon, again, somewhere in my journey, my focus changed. As soon as I began to feel all those things (loved, secure and cherished), I then wanted an even more intimate relationship with the Lord for His sake, no longer it being about me.

That's when I began to ponder just why God created all of us—God created mankind to fellowship with Him. Someday when the new heaven and new earth is created this is what we will all do continually, an earth that has no sorrow, sickness or tears. Is it good enough for our Lord and Savior to wait until each of us leaves this earth to begin our fellowshipping with Him as we were created to do? I knew it was not good enough, not when I pondered what He'd already given to me.

My deepest desire became to be to Jesus what He deserved and longed for—to fellowship with Him in a deep and intimate way. I wanted to be, in this moment of time, like Adam (who walked with God in the "cool of the day"), like Enoch (who was taken up to heaven; maybe because God enjoyed his company so much), and like Moses (who spoke to Him face-to-face, so much so that Moses' face "shone like the sun"). This was now what I wanted and yearned for.

Though I know I am nothing and am certainly unworthy to be a proper companion for Jesus, God could certainly make me to become what He wanted me to be if only I asked. So I asked Him to show me, to teach me, and to make me the Lord's companion, the bride that He desired and so richly deserved.

As a result of my asking, many things happened over the course of the next several months; some of which I remember, and some of which God will have to bring back to my memory if they are things that I am supposed to share with you. The main thing that happened, the turning point, was when I began to tell Him that He was all I wanted, and that He was all that I needed, as I mentioned in the last chapter.

It may not be necessary for you to experience all that God led me through for you to reach this pinnacle where your life changes forever. If you have not yet begun to say these words to the Lord, please begin right now. Just to encourage you, for a very long time I never *felt* those words, but soon you will see, as I did, that your focus will change, and with it, your heart.

Then get ready. Once you have changed enough, God will do something that will turn your life upside down. If you are listening, if you have spent sufficient time in your prayer closet, time alone with Him, you will know all about what's up ahead long before it happens. Giving you enough time so you will not be shaken. "'For the mountains may be removed and the hills may shake, but My lovingkindness will not be removed from you, and My covenant of peace will not be shaken,' says the Lord who has compassion on you." Isaiah 54:10. He will show you, before it happens, that your world, as you know it, is about to fall just as He did with me. "Do not tremble and do not be afraid; have I not *long since **announced** it to you and declared it?* And you are My witnesses! Is there any God besides Me, Or is there any other Rock? I know of none" (Isaiah 44:8).

The reason your life is about to fall is because our very foundation was created and has been held together by us. Yet our desire, and His desire, is to give you a new life. The very foundation that He is about to give you: His life for you, His foundation, which will be high on the Rock, above your enemies, is where He will put that "new song in your heart, a song of praise to our God!"

"To find your life,
You've got to lose it,
All the losers get a crown."

The moment my world fell, when I lost my life, I found the One that God created me for. The difference is as significant as the difference between this world and heaven. My journey and my focus now, is to begin to share with women everywhere, like you dear one, how to find and to live the abundant life that He has created for you to live.

It is no longer enough for me to want this life for myself, and to be the "companion" for our Heavenly Husband as I know He deserves and longs for. I *long* to be His lover, ***and*** I want to draw as many passionate lovers to Him as possible—as many as I can, and for as long as I live this life that He has given me here on earth.

What you will find, as you venture upon this "journey of a lifetime" is a life that explodes with JOY that is truly unspeakable. It is every promise hoped for, now lived. It is beyond anything that you have even hoped for, cried for, or could have ever even imagined. All that you have becomes nothing in comparison to what you are about to receive through your relationship with the Lover of your soul, and from the hand of Him who *longs* for you!

I pray that this chapter, too, will create an even greater yearning that is so deep, and a desire that is so passionate, that you will begin to tell the Lord just how you (want to) feel about Him. Each time you hurt, you are bewildered, you are alone, or you feel you just cannot go on, you need to get to a quiet place (even if that is the quietness of your own mind when there is noise surrounding you) and tell Him that HE is all you want and HE is all that you need.

Tell Jesus that since you have Him, you have everything that you will ever need to make you happy, secure, loved, and complete.

In closing, let me share some more words from the song that I opened with.

"In your weakness, He is stronger,
In your darkness, He shines through.
When you're crying, He's your comfort,
When you're all alone, He's CARRYING you!"

Chapter 3

The Love of My Life

For just as the body without the spirit is dead,
so **also faith without works** is dead.
—James 2:26

When I hosted the luncheon at my home for restoring marriages (and each time I have had the pleasure of ministering to members of my church), I have seen that there are very few who really have the kind of relationship with the Lord that I am experiencing now. When women who I would consider very spiritual talk about their husbands or former husbands, they would often be on the verge of tears, because of their longing for him, or if they were talking about their marriage restoration, they would be almost giddy with the thought. This showed me that their heart was *not* for the Lord, but was very much still for their husband or FH.

God also sees your heart as you *long* for someone other than His Son, and it has to grieve Him even more than it grieves me. I want so much to get this across to every woman in the world—oh, precious one; there is NO REASON for you to hurt, not ever. There is no reason for you to *long* for a man who is longing for the world and the things of this world. You have a special Someone who will cherish and love you, and give you every desire of your heart and if you have enough of Him, you will never experience that pain of rejection or longing again.

The One I am speaking about is right now on bended knee with a proposal on His lips! He does not want you to be His wife, He longs for you to be His Bride—forever!! A bride and a wife are two very different things. A bride is cherished, is new, and is someone very much *in* love! A wife is more of a helpmeet and a "completer." When we are married, we are told to complete and help our husbands. The Bible tells us that, and you have learned that as well in *A Wise Woman;* but God wants something more for you. He longs for you to be the LORD's Bride.

Recently, I was able to explain about this kind of love with my FH when he, once again, asked me about marrying him. Our divorce has been final for not even two months, but this conversation has crept up so often and I confess it makes me sad because I know he simply can't understand what's happened to me. What I am not at liberty to explain is that though I am to be agreeable, the Lord told me there is a reason why I cannot marry again, which I believe is because I now belong to Him (at least for this season in my life).

During these intense conversations, my FH has continued pressuring me to help him to be happy again, to take him back, to forgive him. I told him that of course I forgive him, and I am delighted that we are good friends, but even though he SAYS he loves me, it is not real love. I told him that the love he has is selfish, not because *he* is necessarily selfish, because we all are. That each of us only cares what makes us happy, not what would make others happy.

My FH wants me to give up my happiness that I now have with the Lord in order to make him happy and that's what he calls love. But that is not real love, not the kind that I get from the Lord, nor what he could experience with the Lord if given the opportunity. The kind of love I have now is what I was able to give to my FH during all the recent divorce proceedings.

The love that I gave him (because I had received it from the Lord) was not selfish, but simply giving unselfishly. It enabled me to "cheerfully" give him the divorce that he wanted (for God loves a cheerful giver) because He gives to us in this way. It enabled me to let go of my husband because he said he wanted another woman. And in the area of our finances, because He gave to me, I was able to enthusiastically take our entire family's debt (that was hundreds of thousands that had been hidden from me) that I had no idea how I could ever pay, but I simply trusted that He would certainly give me what I needed.

The love that the Lord gives me enabled me to willingly take the responsibility of our five children who all still live at home, give him joint custody so he can take them whenever he wants, and sign divorce papers that will require me to discuss with him any decision that will affect them (and without a doubt most of the decisions I make will affect our children).

This kind of love goes beyond what is asked and then gives more than what is asked for. It means giving my children to the other woman (time and friendship with her) and encouraging this relationship because that was what my FH wanted me to do. And this list of wants increases daily.

Once again, just this week, my FH told me that he is now so destitute that he has no idea what he is going to do. He said that he would be willing to home-school our children for me, and be a "house-husband" cooking meals and keeping the house clean if only I'd take him back. Unfortunately, I assured him that I could not have the kind of marriage he proposed, but thanked him for being so kind and humble.

When my FH told me how much he still loved me and begged me to forgive him so we could remarry, I told him that I most certainly forgave him for everything and that there was nothing he did or would do that would change my favorable feelings for him. However, he did not love me with the kind of love that I am getting now and that he could only find in the One who loved him as much as He loved me. And the love he said he had for me was a selfish love that every human possesses. And explained that the love he now is feeling from me, and was able to express towards him since he first said that he wanted a divorce and to leave me, is the kind of love that only the Lord can give.

I told him that when he wanted a divorce, because he said it would make him happy, I cheerfully gave it to him. When he wanted me to take over all the debt and responsibility of caring for the children, I gave it gladly to him. When he told me that the *AW was the one who made him happy, I gave him to her and helped him have a better relationship with her. Then when he wanted to create a good relationship between my children and the AW who would be their stepmom, I encouraged it and did what I could to help them to like her.

> *AW: During my first Restoration Journey I referred to the other woman using OW, which interestingly also means "ouch" because knowing about her hurt so much. This time, however, it didn't hurt at all, due to how I was well surrounded in His love. So instead I simply referred to her as just "another woman" hence me using AW instead.

I told him that this is the way that God has loved me. That He gave me all that I wanted and needed, withholding nothing. And it was because I had His kind of love flowing through me, that I was able to give that unselfish and giving love to him.

The selfish love that humans possess leads them to want their own happiness and not care about someone else's happiness, which is what he doesn't understand he's still doing by pressuring me to give up what I now have in my life. What I have now is pure joy and happiness from being with the Lord—He is all I want and all I need, and I told my FH that.

My FH was very quiet and very somber when I finished speaking. Then he apologized for wanting to again get the life that he wanted at the expense of taking mine, and he said that he understood what I was saying. I am not sure if he really understood, but his tone changed after we spoke. My hope is that this prompts him to really want what I have: a relationship with the Lord that will change him from the inside and nothing will shake it.

The truth is my FH thought that leaving me and being with his high school sweetheart would make him happy. And because I withheld nothing, but willingly gave everything (the way the Lord is giving me everything), he instantly gained what he thought he wanted and found that once again, he came up short. He is even more miserable and now he has turned back on the other woman. Now he wants me again once he saw my sheer joy in the midst of everything he put me through, and the blessings I am now experiencing on my life.

It's because I know I am not what he needs, any more than the other woman is. Like him, all men need Jesus just as much as all women do, but instead they look to women, sports, money, fame, etc., all of which leave a man feeling empty, just as empty as the women who look to their husbands (or just men in general) and all the things of this world to make them happy!

The Lord is showing me that whether married or not, EVERY woman needs to be yearning and longing for Him. This is the message that I keep sharing with my daughters and the young women whom I minister to in my church. I hope to plant a seed and the desire to gain this very special and lifelong intimacy with the Lord **now** so that they will not turn their eyes and hearts toward their husbands (to fulfill their needs and desires), but to share each "secret of their hearts" with the Lord not only now, but forever.

When they are faithful to the Lord and keep running after Him **only**, they will glow with the radiance of a new bride all their married lives! And that as long as they pursue the Lord, and not their husbands, their husbands will pursue them (but never overtaking them) for their hearts will be fixed on Jesus! And that if they turn their hearts toward their husbands, that their husbands will assuredly turn their hearts back to pursuing other things (the world, an OW, hobbies, outside friendships or work).

This is my message to all women, young and old, and the message that I will spend the rest of my life sharing with everyone who will listen! My God will supply all of our needs! And one of our greatest needs as a woman is to have intimacy with someone who will love us unselfishly and that person is Jesus, our Heavenly Husband.

So what will happen with all the men of the world if the women begin to have this kind of relationship with the One who created us? I believe that it will certainly get their attention! I believe that once women STOP pursuing men, men will become uneasy. I believe that the world, and the other things that they are pursuing, will no longer have the same thrill that it once had.

I also believe that once our precious Beloved knows that He has our hearts that He will happily begin turning the hearts of our men back to us, and they will be in hot pursuit of us! I have seen this happen in my own life, and in the lives of the ladies in our church who are beginning to grasp this powerful concept and to walk it out in their own lives!!

And as we walk it out, we will be radiant with a heavenly glow because all the fear and pain will be removed from our faces, and we will radiate with the love of the Lord!! This will draw all women to love the Lord as we do, and then turn the men, who will want their women back, toward God and a relationship with His Son!

Yet, even if they want us, they should never get us (at least they will not get me!). Every love song that I hear now, I sing to the Lord (and I sing it out loud when I am in the car alone!). I love to speak sweet nothings each time I think of Him, all day long, especially when I am getting ready for bed, when I slip into bed, and when I wake up in the morning.

I can't wait to get my morning coffee so that I can go to a quiet place alone with Him and share my coffee while I listen to my Beloved speaking to me each morning. Then I sit down to write to my closest friends through emails to tell them how wonderful my Lover is (just like I am doing now with you)! My life is to be envied, even though in our world I have lost just about everything. My hope in writing this book is to create an overpowering yearning and longing in each of your hearts to have the same thing!

I'd love to know that you are having a similar conversation with Him all day long, everyday, because you finally realize He is right there next to you. Rather than thinking of things you need to do, you instead ask Him to take care of everything because He IS your Husband! And guess what? He will! I am still learning all this relationship has to offer— because after all, I am a new bride.

When I was ministering to a single (never been married) young lady just the other day, I explained that with this kind of "love affair" with the Lord going on in a marriage (which needs to be developed *before* marriage), no women would ever have to suffer!

Imagine it, if you will, as a huge banquet of food set before you Are you going to go hungry if the peanut butter sandwich you normally eat is not there? What if your bank account was in the millions, would you even miss a ten-dollar check that someone did not give you? That is what it is like when you have all of Jesus! You will never need or want anything from anyone else. Instead, you can share your food (which never runs out like the loaves and fishes) with everyone who is hungry. You can share your riches with everyone who is poor. You can give your love to your children or husband without *needing* their love to be returned. This is the way God intended us to live, and the reason why He sent His Son to be our Husband: to live, die and hold the keys to death, dying, tears, pain, and shame.

Conclusion

There's no question that our world today is impoverished and it is up to us to feed them with the truth. However, we cannot express to anyone what we don't have ourselves, when we live in poverty and in need! We need to first feast on the intimacy that is ours when we just take the time to develop it. Nothing comes from *thinking* about it—it comes from prioritizing our lives by first prioritizing our hearts!

God is about to shake up the women of the world and I want to be the first in line to follow Him. When I was thinking of heaven (I was singing a song about living in the Father's house where there are many rooms), I told the Lord that I wanted the room closest to His. I told Him not to be surprised if I slept right there by His door, because I couldn't bear being too far away. And that I would rather sleep at the foot of His bed, if He would allow me, like a little puppy who adored its master rather than the most comfortable bed in heaven.

The truth is, I am not really interested in throwing my crown at His feet (though He deserves it) or to hear "well done, my good and faithful servant." I am only interested in that long embrace with Him that I hope will last for all eternity.

—————— Chapter 4 ——————

Give it Away

Give, and it will be **given** to you.
A good measure, **pressed** down, shaken together
and running over,
will be poured into your lap.
For with the measure you use,
it will be measured to you.
—Luke 6:38

Right now I am in a slight financial crisis, so what better time than now to share the awesome principle that God is teaching me in my life? Most of you who face divorce and separation will also encounter financial crises, as they seem to go hand-in-hand. And with the financial crisis, fear uses it as an open door to torment you, and to attack your faith. This I speak of from personal experience.

The good news is, if we simply understand and embrace the principle of *giving* in the **midst** of your need, you will find, as I did, that God really designed trials to **increase** what you have, not simply to *test* your faith. Let me put it this way: when there is a "lack" in your finances (or any other area of your life), God wants you to give (as He leads you), so that He can **increase** what you have.

Of course, our flesh wants to do the opposite; when we are in need we tend to hide or hoard what we have. So like all things spiritual, we need to kill the flesh (by not feeding it) and instead walk in the spirit, so the spirit and our faith will increase. With this truth, you will now have the ability to change your state of mind, so that whenever there is a *lack,* you will rejoice knowing that God has designed this need in order to bring about an *increase* into your life!!

When my husband announced he was divorcing me, he also told me that he was going to leave me all the family debt (much that was hidden), and that he would not pay child support. Ladies, when you are being backed into the Red Sea, which, may I say I found is a wonderful place to be, it is not the time to panic. It just means God is about to show up! I honestly prefer these major crises to the other minor ones because I can easily see that God is Who set me up. I used to think that it was the devil or some other such nonsense (such as the other person who was out to get me). And due to this ignorance, I can't imagine how many times I missed one of God's blessings since I fought against it—all the while He was trying to bless me. I'm still not sure, but I can't remember anyone ever teaching me this principle, is it due to no one really understanding it?

So, let's make this clear, when you are faced with a *lack* or if you find someone who may appear to be pushing you into some sort of lack— don't fight it and please don't panic; instead rejoice—God is about to bless you! The verse that taught me what to do was this, "But I say to you, do **not** resist an evil person; but whoever slaps you on your right cheek, turn the other to him also. If anyone wants to sue you and take your shirt, let him have your coat also. Whoever forces you to go one mile, go with him two" (Matthew 5:38–40).

Yet, even though Jesus told us what we should do, we instead want to hang onto our shirt or try to hide it. And God help us, we are not about to go one more mile! On the contrary, even Christians seek an attorney to hide money and maybe even try to get something from the other person who is in turn trying to get what we have. That's what an attorney is paid to do, which is why I am so grateful Erin taught me early on to simply trust the Lord to fight our battles and release attorneys.

Let's face it, when we act like the world does, we are showing our ignorance to God's Word and His ways, and also proving that we are not His children, because if we were, we would not act so unbecomingly! And once we do act the way that is befitting an heir of our heavenly Father, we will prove to be so unusually strange that we cannot help but draw the lost to notice and soon they become believers in Jesus. Can you believe this added bonus to our increase?! This is what it means to "witness" to the lost, not handing them a track or reciting the Roman's Road to salvation. The lost need to witness how we live differently.

So after each situation of need or lack that has recently been hitting me from every side, and also acknowledging with my lips, "God You're about to bless me!" I can then go to my prayer closet to speak to the Lord to know just how He wants me to handle each situation.

For instance, last week I received papers from our accountant that stated that we (which is now "I" since I agreed to take the debt) owe *thousands* in back taxes. As crazy as it sounds, I was quite excited to see what God was about to do since I knew He had set the entire thing up just to show me how powerful and faithful He is. The Lord loves to be praised, and just like any husband, He wants me to know just how wonderful He is as my Husband since I am now His *new* bride (at least I feel like a new bride)!

Also, knowing how finances (or the lack thereof) can easily bring in fear, I did not read the pages and pages of paperwork too carefully, and instead I left them on my desk until the following morning so that I would have ample time to discuss them with the Lord. I wanted to know what He wanted me to do, and certainly not to come up with a plan (not my plan nor anyone else's, which is why I also never discuss my problems with anyone!). Let us never forget that with each and every trial, test, temptation, or crisis, God already has a plan in place that includes a blessing at the end. He does not want us to think up our own plan on how to get out. Instead, He simply waits for us to come to Him, not in a state of panic or pleading, but in utter trust just as a child would go to a father who could (and would) fix anything!

It was in my prayer closet when the Lord assured me that He had me "covered" and that He would lead me every step of the way regarding my taxes. Without actually saying it, He reminded me of what had happened just weeks earlier when I began following these principles: when I *gave* when I did not have anything (and only because He provided the ability to give once I told Him I would), and then He blessed me with an unexpected blessing of thousands of dollars!

" Rapid-fire memories "

Now back to the back taxes. The next morning, He led me to get my checkbook and to begin reading carefully through the papers that listed all the different checks for the federal and state back taxes owed. At each flip of the page, the amount continued to grow until I realized that I owed tens of thousands that would wipe out that beautiful safety net (the thousands of dollars remaining in my bank account), and while reading, I could hear the Lord whisper, "Do you trust me?" and I smiled with my answer, which was "Of course!"

So He led me to write out one check after another. When I was done, He led me to leave the checks there on my desk. That night and the next morning, each time I would think about the back taxes, I would tell my Beloved that He was all I wanted, He was all I needed and how much I loved and adored Him. The next morning, when I was about to put all the checks into the proper envelopes to mail, God opened my eyes to the fact that I could not write these checks out of the church account as I had, but that they were personal taxes that I needed to pay out of our personal account! If this amount could wipe out that large safety net in our church account, there was no way I had that kind of money in my personal account!

Yet when I told the Lord this, He simply asked me again if I trusted Him and told me, "It is there."

Ladies, we are asked to believe what we do not see, and trust God for each miracle *by faith,* therefore I did believe even though I "saw" I had nothing, and God was again wonderfully faithful! The Lord led me again to calmly write out one check at a time from my personal account, until finally there was only one check left to pay. That was when He led me to stop. When I did, I realized it was the largest check and that I had actually written the other checks "out of order" of their due date. That's when the enemy tried to hound me about leaving this one unpaid and primarily torment me about paying the debts "out of order." Yet I went ahead and left that one debt for almost a week until the Lord led me back to the papers and my checkbook.

When the ordeal was all said and done, I had paid **all** of our back taxes out of my personal account!! There is no way that was possible—no way!! But He made a way, though I cannot explain how He did it!

So, when facing my new financial crisis this week, all of my own testimony ran through my mind, when once again, I was pressed back to the Red Sea. I am sure that it was the after-effect of the back taxes, but this week when it came time to pay the mortgage payment for our home, I knew it was not there. I had nothing at all. What was sad, but made me laugh, was that I didn't even have enough to pay for a field trip for my three youngest children—a total of just $6.00 (I hope you are laughing too)! I had just finished writing out payroll checks and paying the church bills, and that was when I came face-to-face with the Red Sea again.

What also made me laugh was that this was one area that my FH had mocked me on and that he kept telling me would happen. He had even made it a point to tell our older children that I was going to "lose the house" with my "foolish giving" that I had *foolishly* claimed was "faith." Of course I never tried to defend myself because Lord knows I **am** a fool. 1 Corinthians 1:27 says, "For God has chosen the foolish of the world to shame the wise, and He has chosen the weak of the world to shame the mighty." Yep, that's me.

Though I normally try to do all the accounting on Saturdays, I had no idea what to do. So when I do not know what to do, I do nothing; I do not even think about what to do. Again, I left the checkbook and bills and went upstairs to rest in the Lord and in His goodness. I took every opportunity to get alone with the Lord, not so He could reassure me, nor so I could cry or plead, because I was actually full of joy and excitement. I got alone with Him simply to affirm my love for Him and His for me—telling Him that He was all I wanted and all that I needed. It was near the end of each of our little rendezvous when the Lord would tell me "It's there," meaning that the money was there. I know that I did not know *where* it was hidden, but if He said it was there, He would show me how to find it.

Let me interject that God has done wonders in building my faith. I have seen Him do the incredible, and to increase my faith, I spend lots of time every day thinking about each time He has come through and blessed me. "Counting" and listing my blessings, one-by-one each day is what lulls me to sleep, and it's also how I wake up each morning by repeating them again. I do it to renew my mind, and in all my time alone with Him I also love to tell Him how wonderful this or that was.

In addition, I never keep exciting things to myself. I also find many opportunities to tell others about each miracle He has done. And because I have five children, I like to tell them each separately. Because each time I speak about it, it increases my faith (and theirs) and it also gives God the glory He deserves. So often when God comes through for us, we barely acknowledge that it happened. This weakens our faith rather than builds it. Those who send praise reports to RMI, which by the way I love to read, and who make a point of telling others of God's faithfulness, are those who see great and mighty things in their lives! So when God does something, think back when you did not know what you would do, and then how perfectly He worked it out for you. Think of it over and over and over again, and use each opportunity to increase other people's faith by sharing your testimony each time God gives you the opportunity. This also fulfills the principle of giving away when you're in need, and also is "witnessing." So if you need more faith, give away what you have by sharing what He's done for you in the past.

So, it was the next morning, which was a Sunday, when I woke up in my usual way by telling the Lord how happy He makes me and how much I loved Him and listing everything wonderful He did for me the day before, when God brought something to my mind. He reminded me that when my FH moved away, he had asked for "a loan," which wiped me out financially (making it impossible to meet our payroll. By the way, I did not "loan" the money to him, but instead I told him that it was a gift he did not have to pay back). That week, because there wasn't enough, He told me not take a paycheck (or I would *not* have been able to pay our employees). But then I remembered, I still had my huge safety net (it was still there, remember, because I miraculously paid all the back taxes from my personal account!). Therefore, just as the Lord had said, the money was there! I simply paid myself a back paycheck owed to me, but in my mind, as I quickly calculated it, I would *still* be short—but I wasn't! I was able to pay all (not just some) of our family's personal bills. Though it has been more than 24 hours since this miracle occurred, I am still blown away and I can't figure out how He did it!! It's impossible. Mark 10:27, "Looking at them, Jesus said, 'With people it is impossible, but not with God; for **all** things are possible with God.'"

Before I had paid my house payment, the Lord had led me to write a very large check to our African Missionaries, and still there was more than enough in my personal account! Later, knowing that I needed to increase what I had (not just get the bills paid), I asked God how else He wanted me to give. Immediately, I remembered that one of my sons was in need of a comforter set for his bedroom. So, while running errands a few days ago, I had seen masculine comforters at a nearby store, and I remembered that when we had moved into our new home, this son was the only one who did not get a new comforter set for his bed. So after church, I headed to the store that the Lord had placed in my mind. I knew I would find just what I needed, which I did. And later when I told my son what I had bought for him, he told me that this was something he kept thinking that he needed to get, but he did not have the money for it, so he had trusted God to provide. God wanted to bless him, and He chose to use me!

Since there is still a need in my bank account, and I know that God brought this need in order to, once again, increase what I have, I will continue to look for opportunities to give. Many different ideas have come into my mind, but I will simply wait and allow the Lord to begin opening the doors to the ones that are His idea and not mine. What I love is that we do not have to make things happen, all we have to do is to walk toward the doors that the Lord illuminates in our minds or hearts, and then wait for Him to open the door (as a Gentleman would). And if a door does not open, just keep moving towards another open door. Never, ever force a door open—His ways are effortless; the only effort will be in exercising your faith.

Testimony: More Giving

The principle of giving when you are in need is not just applicable to finances and money, it also holds true for every area of your life. When I was feeling the effects of being a "single mom of five," my son asked me about his friend moving in for a week since he had nowhere to go. Within a few hours, my daughter's friend found that she was locked out of her house because her mom was away for almost two weeks, so I suggested that she stay with us. That's because I knew that God was about to increase my strength and stamina, and I wanted to work *with* God!

That same week, my brother who lives in Asia had for some unknown reason, not gotten my emails that his daughter could **not** come live with us for a year to go to school, and he was pressing me to make the arrangements for her flight! Once I cooperated with what the Lord was doing, I found myself with strength and stamina that I did not know I had! In my need, God brought opportunities to give away what little strength I had left in order to give me the increase I needed!! And now whenever I have financial troubles, I know that I need to watch for what God wants me to do to give away what little I have left.

God showed me this principle many years ago when I was breastfeeding my babies. The more my babies nursed, the more milk I had. Many doctors or lactation specialists will sadly tell a mother that she needs to supplement with formula and that she does not have enough milk when her baby is fussy and wants to nurse all the time! But the truth is that God made that perfect baby and gives the mother all the food for her growing baby. Though I had doctors telling me that I would have to supplement (since I had huge babies, one close to 12 pounds at birth), I knew that I would have enough milk **if** I just would sit still and let my baby nurse as much as he wanted at each growth spurt!

Not only did I not have to supplement my baby's diet with formula, I was able to donate my excess milk to a neonatal hospital. At one point they asked me to help a little girl who could only tolerate my milk. So the hospital sent out a cab to pick up my milk each day. During this crisis, I decided to feed my baby one side and gave the milk from the other side to the hospital. Months later, I received a picture of the healthy little girl who was well enough and able to go home to her family.

✦ God wants to do great things when we trust Him enough to give away what we naturally want to hang onto or hoard because we fear that we will not have enough.

As I keep saying, this principle works in every area of your life: finances, love, strength, and time—the list is endless. When you begin to notice a "lack" in any area of your life, this is when God is saying, "I am about to increase what you have! Now, put your faith to work for you. Believe what you don't see, walk in that faith. Don't pull back; don't begin to fear that you will run out. I am your Source, but I need your faith, shown by your works (walking it out) for this spiritual law to manifest itself."

And walking out your faith does not mean that you say, "Let me give this, this and this," but instead, watch for the opportunities that the Lord brings and sets before you. They will be large and small. One morning, I saw an opportunity to bless a teen (whom I know needs Jesus) with a cup of Starbucks coffee. When she resisted, I was able to share with her how God loves to bless us and that I was excited when God showed me areas where I could bless others! So she took it understanding where my Source is, and where hers could be too. There are so many who need to see evidence in order to understand the goodness of God, but how will they know if they don't see it first hand in our lives?

In the midst of all this giving, I had a situation come up that I had to go to God for understanding. I actually went to Him to repent, since I thought I had missed an opportunity to give. A woman came up to me and wanted my business card, but I hesitated and I asked her why she wanted it. She told me that she wanted to get to know me and to call me sometimes just to talk. I told her that I am so busy with my five children (and my niece) and that when I am home (and not traveling), I have very little time for any social life. And as a matter of fact, I had to cancel an appointment with a dear friend because I was home-schooling my youngest three in the morning. Thankfully, I was interrupted by another friend who came up to say hi so the woman simply walked away.

When I spoke to the Lord about it, repenting, He told me that He had led me to resist this woman's efforts because it was the enemy who comes to steal from us and wear out His children. He told me that though He puts out opportunities for us to give, the enemy is also right there to steal or to simply wear us out. When I asked Him how we know when it is Him and not the enemy, He said that when we stay close to Him, we will instinctively, in our spirits, discern His leading and will naturally not fall prey to it.

Another way we fall prey is when we begin to become prideful about our giving. Our testimonies no longer praise God, but praise us (and how generous and giving we are)! This will ultimately be the net for us to fall into or a podium for us to fall off of. So be very careful when you share your testimony. Make sure that it is the Lord you are lifting up and not your greatness.

Also, look for opportunities to give, but don't just run around giving. God needs to present opportunities to you and open the door for it to bring His increase. There are times when we might see a need, but God doesn't want us to fill it. It might be that the need is for someone else to fill or it may be that the lack is what God is using to get the other person to cry out to Him. And as God told me, staying close to Him will give us the greatest protection of doing it just right!

So once again, take some time to fall in love with your Lover today and this week. Tell Him that He is all you want and all that you need. Sing your favorite love song to Him and remind yourself of all the ways that He has blessed you. No one needs to live a life of lack when our God, and our Husband, is the ultimate Source for everything that never runs dry!

Chapter 5

It's SO Worth the Wait

For the vision is yet for the appointed time;
It hastens toward the goal and it will not fail
Though it tarries, **wait for it**;
For it will certainly come, it will not delay.
—Habakkuk 2:3

This morning, I began to read in my Bible, especially in Psalms, all the verses that I had highlighted since the Lord restored my marriage in 1991. Next to these Scripture verses, I wrote a "PF" meaning Promise Fulfilled! Though I spent over an hour reading these and marking these verses, I did not come across even one that the Lord had not fulfilled!!

Reading and marking them PF gave me time to reflect and to go back to all those days when it seemed that God would never show up! Years of crying out to Him, years when I thought today (when I would recognize that each and every one of those promises He has fulfilled) would never arrive. Precious one, if I am not mistaken, that is where most of you who are reading this book are right now. You have believed for better days, better times, and have truly put your trust in the Lord, but you are still waiting, waiting, waiting . . .

Will you ever reach the place of peace, prosperity, and (could you ever even imagine?) joy in your life? YES! I was where you are right now for years, and years, and years! If I really take time to look back over my life, I probably have been in this place for close to...well, my math is not that good this early in the morning! My entire life has been hard. My best friend, whom I have known since the eighth grade, says that she knows no one who has lived anything close to what I have lived through. But because I have traveled, and I personally know so many of you who are in my fellowship, I also know there are many of you who have gone through much worse. But I guess I have been through enough to tell you that, YES, indeed it is worth the wait—and your wait has a wonderfully planned purpose!

As I look back, it was the waiting that made me into whom I am today. The wait enabled me to know the Lord the way that I do now. I would never have known Him as intimately, and I would never have been able to appreciate Him, or my life, like I do now, surely not in the way that I needed to know Him. I would not have been able to minister to ladies, not as I am able to do now. I thought that through my prior marriage restoration is how I would be able to minister most effectively. So that when I lost my restored marriage, I thought my ministering to women was over. Yet like all brokenness it's been through my recent divorce that I have been able to minister to countless more women! And some of the "why" I've had for so long has finally been answered. Back then I believed that my ministry was based on my restored marriage, and as a result, that is what the women I ministered to also wanted, what I had—a restored marriage. Yet now, today, women see my joy and my abundant life, and now they want what I now have—my Beloved in full measure! Oh, can we ever doubt His ways or feel faint (or heaven forbid) give up without **waiting** for all of His precious promises to be fulfilled?!

The good news for all of you ladies and every woman in this world is that you do not have to wait for the joy, peace or prosperity (or even love) that you yearn for from a man or from things or positions. Though it took me years to get to this place in my life, those years were only so that God could use me to help build you a super-highway or bullet-train to your desired haven through my years of pioneering the rough road so many women travel and fall prey to. This freeway's name is Jesus, our Beloved Husband, and He will carry you to your promises in His arms of love! You may have to wait for all your promises to be fulfilled, but the waiting room that He has designed for you is suited for a woman just like you. Interested? Then follow me as we learn why God purposely designed waiting to bring us the promises that He has every intention of giving us once He knows that we are truly *ready* to handle them.

Why We Wait

Waiting for something is one of the hardest aspects of the Christian walk; we simply do not know how to do it properly. Rather than benefiting from it, and enjoying it, we suffer through it; often failing to make it to the end and thus we forfeit the promise we are trusting God for.

Yet the Bible is clear that when God shows us something, when we cry out to Him, it is yet for an *appointed time*, it is (usually) not for now. Habakkuk 2:2-3, "Then the LORD answered me and said, 'Record the vision and inscribe it on tablets, that the one who reads it may run. For the vision is yet for the appointed time; it hastens toward the goal and it will not fail. Though it tarries, WAIT for it; for it will certainly come, it will not delay.'" And this is why He also tells us to write it down, so we can read it often, knowing He is faithful.

Understanding why we wait may be even more important than believing for the promise itself. Simply put, when God shows us something for the future, it is because we are not ready to deal with it, or to enjoy it fully, without this intended period of waiting.

Consider the life of Joseph. He was just a boy when he saw the vision that he would rule and that his own family would one day bow down to him. However, he needed many years to mature, during which time he would have to suffer and grow spiritually before he would be ready for the responsibility or the position that he was destined for. There was nothing that he could do to hurry it up, or make God think he was ready, for his promise to be made manifested and seen.

Then there is Moses. He was a young man when he ran away to the desert, and many years of seclusion from public life passed before he was ready to lead the millions to the Promise Land.

Consider, Esther, she was nowhere near ready to be queen until she first grew in understanding her people, the Jews, under the tutelage of her cousin, Mordecai. She also needed a full year of beauty preparation for her to summon her husband, the king, who would normally have executed her for such an act. God knew that she was not ready to face the enormous task of saving her Jewish people, let alone reveal her true identity as a Jew herself.

Yet the wait is not only for **our** good, it is also because often the timing is not right. God orchestrates each person and event to come together at an exact moment in time for His glory. We tend to forget this part, due to our naturally self-centered and self-absorbed self. All we know is that **we** are tired of waiting, all the while forgetting that the Lord is soon to be glorified and it's for this reason God is bringing this miracle in our lives anyway.

In my own situation, it took many years for me to be emotionally and spiritually ready, as well as being in the right place for God to bring all of His promises to me and into the light for others to see. Though I once wished that it would have been sooner, I can see now that nothing was ready even a day sooner than it happened. But let's talk about the time in between the waiting times that are often the times when we are suffering, which leads to our wondering if God really cares.

Is that not what this is all about?

When we suffer and our situation does not change, it's then that we begin to doubt God's love for us. We wonder if He cares about us as much as someone else who we look at who did not have to wait as long as we have been waiting. We begin to wonder if what we have asked God for, and believed God for, is even in His will anyway. And with this kind of negative and faith-destroying thought, we very often simply walk away and leave His promise behind, moving on, instead to something that we can attain right **now**. Then when our original promise shows up, we are often nowhere to be found or we could even care less that God has once again been faithful to us. So sad.

That's where most Christians live—it's now or never, and why these same people do their best to get you to live that way too. They only want to believe with you and pray for you for a *reasonable* amount of time, and then if the promise hasn't happened, they do their best to encourage you to doubt that God ever gave you the promise in the first place. Continuing to pray for something that does not show up soon enough is not worth their effort—they have better things to do with their time and prayers.

Let's face it, we live in a "now" lifestyle that goes against God's ways. And even worse than the now lifestyle, is the premature lifestyle that has sprung up. We see it everywhere. Women who are tired of being pregnant are induced; or even if they do wait to begin labor naturally, they will get their labor sped up with drugs or have their water broken. Yes, it is so easy to give into these temptations when you are suffering, with that doctor or nurse standing right there to offer you *immediate* relief.

We do not wait for what we want, even for material things. Today, we do not have to **save** for anything. We can buy everything we want **now**, and pay for it later. Yet this isn't new, it has been going on for ages. Look at Sarah who got her promise for a son through Hagar, but paid for it later. And we are all still paying for Sarah's impatience as we watch the continual wars, violence, hate, and bloodshed in the Middle East between both of Abraham's sons, Ishmael (Islam) and Isaac (Israel). If only Sarah had waited for her promise.

We often forget how our getting ahead of God inevitably affects others, and that is because we are selfish by nature. It is not until we care more about God's will than we do our own will that we really are able to endure to the end. If we could really see what that promise, or those promises together (each and every one spoken to us)—what it will really be like when the right time comes—we could easily endure to the end, and maybe even learn to enjoy the wait.

And what about these thoughts, the vain imaginations? Are vain imaginations detrimental to our walk of faith or are they a way for us to make it to our desired destination? I personally think that they can be both. If we live in the imaginary world too much, we can lose ourselves in it, and often lose our way. But I also personally believe that some imagining can be good, as we are "imagining or believing" what is unseen and doing our best to see our mountain moved. But to live there is to lose sight of God and what He has for us here, during the wait, in the midst of some of the suffering that helps refine us and prepare us.

Looking back, I can see how God created great endurance in me during my long wait and years of different kinds of suffering—all to get me ready for today just like Joseph and Moses. It's only now that I am able to be calm while living an extremely fast-paced life, filled with daily trials that I could not possibly have kept up with or understood in my thirties or even forties. I have no idea how He did it, but that is the point—it is something that HE did, nothing that I could have done, and it all happened during the wait. God is molding you and me moment-by-moment, day-by-day, through each event and circumstance in our lives. Nothing is worthless or unnecessary. It all makes up the training ground and refining fires that prepare us for what He is calling us to do. I believe that most women who are called to serve and be used by Him are too busy to see what God is doing and they often miss the call or are not prepared for it once they are called.

They are also so caught up with the magnitude of the call that they are too afraid to step forward. I venture to say, dear one, that you are one of those ladies. God has given you a vision for your future that is so tremendously incredible that you literally shudder, thinking that it may be true. So you stop thinking about it being enormous, and in turn, instead, you are not embracing what will prepare you, you instead are praying and pleading today's difficulties will change. Is that where you are? I detect that a few tears will fall on these pages as He shines the light into the hidden places of your heart. I know because I was where most of you are right now. And honestly, in some ways, I am again where you are, since God has shown me even greater things that He has planned for me to do that are the new promises that are yet to be—huge, incredible, but yes, scary visions.

Nevertheless, this time I have committed to simply going through everything and this time enjoying the wait. This way I can allow the stretching of my faith, and to make the best use of my time right now during the wait. Each day I stop to look around at each and every thing that God has blessed me with and thank Him for each (as I said earlier in this chapter). And today, this very moment, I am going to take time to look around at the beauty of this world that He has created for His betrothed, you and me. I am going to take the time to love and to cherish those whom God has placed around me, just like He loves and cherishes you and me.

Throughout every day, I am going to take lots of time to tell my precious Beloved how much He is all I want and all that I need. Then when I see the vision for the future or read a promise in my Bible, I will anticipate its coming, and not waste my time wondering if I heard God correctly—no matter how big the promise or vision seems to me now. I will simply believe it because I know God and I know how He works. I know from looking at the millions of things He's already done in my life to know He is faithful. And if you do not think that you have enough faithfulness in your own life, just look at mine (or some of the other women in our fellowship). (And if you are not in our fellowship, you should be, because the women in our fellowship are the ones who keep me going strong!)

Before closing this chapter, let me speak to some of you who are really in the midst of true suffering because I have been there too. First, this suffering really does have a purpose; I do know this from living through it. A broken and contrite heart is not easily obtained by anyone, and it is most certainly painful, but we only need to look at the life of Jesus to understand that He understands and that He is truly "acquainted with our grief." It is sometimes hard for us to understand how God, His Father, could have allowed the kind of suffering of a cross for His only Son. Watching His pleading in the Garden of Gethsemane, but still not stopping it when He heard His Son cry out and writhe and wrestle with what He knew was about to happen, can help us understand because we now can see the outcome of letting His Son accomplish its purpose.

How can a Father watch from heaven while His precious Jesus struggled to carry the cross through the streets that, He knew, would hold His dead body only hours later. (But God did send someone to carry His cross and He has also sent Someone to carry yours too, just ask.) Do you ever wonder how God the Father could watch His only Son on that cross for all those hours during which He suffered and died, and yet why He did not stop the agony and suffering? Did God not see the faces of those who were beaming, those who had been waiting for that day when Jesus of Nazareth would finally die? Did He not hear the insults and mocking being hurled at His Son from the crowd and those who seemed uninterested in this Man's pain, the perfect and sinless man, whom they had just cast lots for His clothing? How could God let this happen? Why did He not stop it, not allowing one more minute to pass? Would the enemy really win, really be able to destroy the good that Jesus did while on the earth?

We all know that the truth is there **was** a purpose, the Purpose that was designed to save you and me. God the Father saw past all the pain, insults, suffering and mocking to peer into our faces, the face of you and me (and your friend, neighbor, brother, sister, mother, father, son and daughter) who needed that precious blood that was falling first from his sweat, then from his crown, later from His scourging, and finally from the nails in His hands and feet—even from His spear-split side. Each and every drop was needed to save you and me. Not one drop was wasted, nor any suffering lost that Jesus and God who was watching, endured for you and me.

Each time you suffer dear one, just as I have, take a moment to remember Jesus and what He did for you and me. How He is helping us now, so that each bit of suffering will also be for a special purpose. Remembering is what has given me the compassion to comfort you right now. You trust me because I have been where you are now, and I really do understand. God does love you and He does care for you. If He was able to let each painful part in history play out for His Son, does He not also have a wonderful plan for you and for others who will benefit due to your willingness to suffer? As I have reached out and comforted you, so you will have women in your world whom I will never meet who also need comfort. No one but you will understand or be able to give them the comfort and hope that they need.

Dear reader, God has a purpose for your wait. Each and every tear you shed is being collected in His bottle. So, now, close this book and go to your prayer closet right away, and let Him comfort you and allow Him to engulf you with His love. He can and will bring peace to your storm, joy to your broken heart, and strength to your weary body and soul. Our Husband, precious one, is just waiting in that quiet place where He wants to wipe away all your tears and all your shame. Go there now and come out ready to comfort others with the comfort that we ourselves have been comforted with by a Living God—our Heavenly Husband.

—————— Chapter 6 ——————

They Don't Have It

They will possess a double portion in their land . . .
I will faithfully give them their recompense.
—Isaiah 61:7–8

Earlier this week the "onslaught of the wicked" hit our home with accusations, mocking, ridicule, cruel words, and condemnation, which inevitably led to fear. Sadly, it was my ex-husband who hurled these attacks at my youngest daughter and at me.

Understandably, my daughter was extremely puzzled, besides being hurt. So once I was able to comfort my daughter, allowing a short time for all sorts of emotions in me to die down, I sought the Lord for wisdom and understanding. He reminded me of what I was writing in this very chapter. God was confirming this principle to me—"they, others, don't have it."

The Lord showed me that the tide of kindness from my ex-husband turned ugly because, for the first time since he first asked for the divorce, he had done *all the asking* and I had done *all the giving*. That day I had foolishly asked for help with three small things: for website links for some health products that he used to use to purchase for the family, for the computer that he was not using so our children could use it for their studies, and to have him initiate some phone calls to the children since they had told me that their dad no longer cared for them. Things turned ugly because I went to him, asking, that turned this once kind man into an angry and fighting man.

The first time God showed me this very important principle, "they don't have it," was at the end of a very long series of frustrating and time-consuming encounters with our warehouse membership club.

It's where I purchased a lot of our groceries and ministry office supplies. There were so many mistakes each time when I tried to make a purchase it became exhausting. As an example, during one incident, it took them over an hour to fix something, all while my frozen foods (that are always in bulk size) melted.

When I went in to shop the next time, I was again at the customer service counter since my membership card was not working. While at the counter, I mentioned the ruined frozen foods from the previous month, whereby the manager apologized and told me to just bring in my receipt for the ruined frozen foods on my next visit, which I did. But instead of a refund, that day's manager told me he also needed the empty boxes for him to be able to give me the refund. That was when I felt myself lose my peace, and instead of bubbling over with kindness and patience, I instead felt frustration and even anger — though, praise God, I did not show it or express it. Nevertheless, just to *feel* this awful emotion was enough for me to be very concerned.

The next time while at the checkout, I was again directed to go to the customer service counter, but this time I was laughing out loud. While they were trying to make sense of why my card was not working correctly, I spoke to the Lord and asked Him when these troubles with my card would all end. He stated very clearly, "When it no longer bothers you." Ouch. So while still standing at the counter, He reminded me of a verse that He had showed me that morning during my time alone with Him. "Instead of your shame you will have a *double* portion, and instead of humiliation they will shout for joy *over their portion*. Therefore they will possess a **double portion** in their land, everlasting joy will be theirs. For I, the LORD, love justice…and *I will* **faithfully give them their recompense**" (Isaiah 61:7–8). Did you see it? He said, *I will.*

Though the Lord did not actually say it, there was an *inner knowing* that I had looked to the wrong source for *my recompense*. It didn't say "They will" but it says, *I will.* **Meaning the Lord will….**

So immediately in my heart I acknowledged again that He was all I wanted **and** all that I needed. I did not need these people or anyone else to make things right or give me any recompense. Even though they had caused me loads of trouble or even that it resulted in hundreds of dollars of damaged frozen foods—I had my Beloved and He was all I needed. At that moment, not only did I stop looking for them to "make it right," I adamantly did not want anything *from* them—I wanted all the blessings of my recompense to come from Him and no one else.

When that feeling began to flow over me, the Lord reminded me that these were Abram's feelings too. It was when the king of Sodom tried to give him a *reward* by giving him the "goods" that were taken when they defeated Chedorlaomer. Abram refused, "Abram said to the king of Sodom, 'I have sworn to the LORD God Most High, possessor of heaven and earth, that I will not take a thread or a sandal thong or anything that is yours, for fear you would say, 'I have made Abram rich'" (Genesis 14:22–23). Abram (who later becomes Abraham) did not want to take away any of God's glory by letting the king take the credit for any of Abram's future wealth, which, as we know, increased **greatly** later in Abram's life—that was secured due to his conviction to give God the glory.

Within about three minutes of this revelation, there at the customer service counter, the Lord did something that was so amazing and funny and incredible just to prove this principle to me. Something I knew I should share with you. In an instant, the woman who was helping me asked me why my card had only a one percent cash-back, instead of a two percent cash-back. I told her that I didn't know that two percent cash-back on purchases was offered. So she turned the computer screen to show me the amount I got back last month, and what I should have gotten with the added percent. The amount doubled! At that point, she immediately changed it and I watched as God gave me a **double recompense,** more than double the cost of the spoiled food. It happened the moment I decided to let the Lord be everything to me once again!

And since He does things above what we ask or think, the next thing I knew was that this same lady began handing me all sorts of their promotional products that they give as gifts to their new customers!! I asked her what she was doing, and she said that it was the least they could do for all the trouble I had been through.

Do you see what happened? As soon as I stopped trying to get satisfaction from the source of my trouble (who "did not have it") and turned to the Lord who is the ultimate Source of all we need, He flooded me with tremendous favor and a multiplied recompense, which He promises to every one of us!

That is what the Lord spoke to me in the car that day on my way home from the warehouse store—they don't have it; they simply do not have it. He said that the people of this world are bankrupt in every way. Think about it. The people of the world (and most Christians) lack compassion, kindness, love, and everyone has limited resources, yet we foolishly keep looking to *them* for our needs. All the while our Lord, our Lover, and our Friend has an endless source of every resource that we need and want—available to us—when we simply look to Him alone!!

And every time we look to others instead of to Him, we find ourselves in even greater **need** when they fail to give us what we may need, deserve or want. That's when we, too, end up bankrupt because by looking to others, we have pulled the plug, cut the tie, severed our Source, Him. "I am the vine, you are the branches; he who abides in Me and I in him, he bears much fruit, for apart from Me you can do nothing" (John 15:5).

So when the Lord brought the principle that "they don't have it" to my mind this week, in reference to my ex-husband, I knew that I had failed to seek what I needed from my true Source. Instead, I had sought what I needed (and what I felt my children needed) from someone who "didn't have it." God showed me that as the Lord's bride, He gives me **more** than I need so I don't need to seek *anything* from *anyone*. Instead, I am expected, as His bride, to *give* to others in need from *my* over-abundance; my overflowing resources. And when we seek from any source who "doesn't have it," we too find ourselves without what we want and need and immediately become selfish and stingy—not a characteristic of the Lord's bride.

When I asked the Lord how to make it right with my ex-husband, He told me simply to wait and that it was all part of His plan. I knew that His plan was to give me more understanding (as I write it down in this chapter), but to also use it in my ex-husband's life to refine and change him so he too can begin experiencing His love. And it's also God's plan for me to explain this principle, teaching it to my children and every woman who reads this book.

The next morning I told the children (who knew about the incident with their dad) that it was entirely my fault. That I had tried to "take" instead of "give" when we had *everything,* because we had God who gave us all we want and all we need, and the Lord was my ultimate Husband and generous Father to them. And that he (their dad), right now, had nothing. And I proceeded to explain the principle of God's giving us a double recompense when we look to Him rather than to others, and the testimony of my experience at the warehouse store.

Within a half of an hour of speaking to my children, my ex-husband called my youngest daughter to make things right. After he spoke to her, he asked to speak to me, and that's when I was able to tell him that the incident the day before was entirely my fault because I should have just turned to the Lord for the things that I needed, instead of asking him. I could tell that he did not want to hear this because he is still trying to find his way back home to me (although he has ceased to pursue me outwardly). This gave me the opportunity, too, to tell my ex-husband how God takes care of all that I need *and* want since the Lord is my Husband now. At that point, my ex-husband tried to give me what I had originally asked him for, beginning with the website links. I thanked him kindly, but said that I did not need them. Then he said that he might be able to give us the computer, but again I said that if we really needed one, God would provide one or the children could simply go to the ministry office to use a computer there.

Then he jumped in, telling me that he wanted to be more available for the children, to which I replied that this was between the children and him, and had really nothing to do with me. I went on to say that I was wrong to try to get a better relationship for them because the one that the Lord had given to us (the children and me) was more than enough for the children, and it shows in the joy that is in our home and that radiates from their faces and voices. That's when the tide had turned back and the pain left my heart, piercing his. Once I put the Lord back in His rightful place in my life, being all I want and all I needed, He then honored me even more!

After lunch, right in the midst of another ministry mini-crisis, I was led to a website I used to use but had forgotten about. There on that *one* site I was able to find *all* of the health products I needed, at a discount, and with reduced shipping (now and in the future)! Since I looked to the Lord alone, He had led me to one website instead of the three or four websites that my ex-husband had used. A few minutes later, I found I had a message on my phone from my ex-husband (that he had left before I spoke to him when I took the blame). The voicemail was a humble apology for my husband's ugliness to my daughter and me, asking for both our forgiveness!

Here is this same principle in a verse most of us can recite, but so few of us can live by on a daily basis: "And *my God* **will supply all your needs** according to His riches in glory in Christ Jesus" (Philippines 4:19). When we tell the Lord that He is all we want and all we need, we need to back it up with our actions and reactions. When someone does us wrong, which seems to happen every day, all day, we need to search our hearts: from whom are we trying to get what we believe we "deserve"—from God or man? God has everything; man has nothing (only what God gives him).

And, yes, it is true that God uses people and circumstances to give us our double recompense. Of course I was grateful and very appreciative of the lady who gave me the double percent cash-back and the promotional gifts, but in my heart I knew who had orchestrated it! I knew, too, who had refined my ex-husband and turned his heart to say that he was sorry.

The exciting addition to this principle is that when we are able to act and react properly, which results in abundance, we can then be channels of God's goodness to others who are in need and who are completely bankrupt. "Many will seek the favor of a generous man, and every man is a **friend** to him who **gives gifts**" (Proverbs 19:6). When we are sought out, and choose to give generously, then we can influence others, by our example, to seek and pursue God to be their Source, which is evangelism and witnessing to others—all without a word.

This is the problem in today's world, in regard to our Christian ineffectiveness; we seem to have a lot to say, but we do not back it up with the way that we act and react to others or deal with our difficult circumstances. This, then, makes us Pharisees. It also mocks God and His goodness, and it results in us being ineffective in evangelism and leading others to want to know Him too. But on the other hand, when we walk this principle out, even when we may mess up a bit like I did, we have a wonderful opportunity to let our light shine and create a saltiness that makes others thirsty for Him! **"Let your light shine** before men in such a way that they may see your good works, and glorify your Father who is in heaven" (Matthew 5:16). **"You are the salt of the earth**; but if the salt has become tasteless, how can it be made salty again? It is no longer good for anything, except to be thrown out and trampled underfoot by men" (Matthew 5:13). If you're being trampled, it simply means you're no longer salty.

"As the deer **pants** for the **water** brooks, so my soul **pants** for You, O God" (Psalm 42:1). Because of my association with many of you who are also RMI partners, my thirst for God continues to grow stronger each and every day. This is the same effect you (if you are salty) will have on those in your world. Our lives should radiate with joy, prosperity, and favor that is envied by all those who know us or know *about* us. It is only then that we can step aside and point to the true Source of our happiness—our Lover and Friend, our Lord and Heavenly Husband.

This Person is only real when we allow Him to be real in our lives, when we truly become His bride. And as His bride, we will want for nothing. This is the message our lives, our lips, and the joy in our hearts that we must tell by how we live—that He, our Beloved, is all that any woman needs. There is no longer any need to run after a man to supply anything for us or to protect us. And not only will our needs be met above and beyond what we could hope, ask, or even think, all of it will come without pain or shame or regrets. Wow!

"Now glory be to God, who by his mighty power at work within us is able to do far more than we would ever dare to ask or even dream of—infinitely beyond our highest prayers, desires, thoughts, or hopes" (Ephesians 3:20 TLB).

"God can do anything, you know—far more than you could ever imagine or guess or request in your wildest dreams!" (Ephesians 3:20 The Message).

The love that you see on television or in movies, or what is sung about in songs, is not real. It is contrived, due to unrelieved pain, shame, and rejection. And sadly, it leaves us in more want and in more need. Unlike the love that is available from our Lover, the source of all love, which has no painful or unwanted side-effects— and the Source never ends!

What about you? Are you still experiencing a need in your life? Then it is only because you have not gone to the true Source of everything.

Do you still experience pain, shame, guilt, condemnation, and tears? Then, dear one, you simply do not have enough of Him. The Lord is calling you to be His bride, not His wife. He wants to lavish you with love, compassion, kindness, and safety from all harm and everything that brings heartache. The only tears that you should shed are those that flow when you ponder how good God is and how He has blessed you.

Take time today, right now, to get even closer and more intimate with your blessed Bridegroom. He is just waiting to embrace you and wipe away your every tear and fear. Precious bride, He loves you!

Quieting Concern

In this and other chapters, I've mentioned that my ex-husband is "still trying to get back home to me" and I felt it necessary to share some insight. Though you or I may want my marriage restored again, what the Lord has shown me (again and again each time I seek Him about this), is that my ex-husband and my children's father needs a true relationship with Him. As a former pastor, and a man well known publically, like many, is openly living in un-repented sin, due to his severed or never established personal relationship with the Lord. And on many occasions has told me God cannot forgive him again, so he's walked away from Him.

And even if some may judge me, I know that Who I need to be sure I am pleasing, is Who I follow and listen to along this new, never before, explored journey.

God allowed my new journey for all of our good, for my children, for me to learn, and especially for my ex-husband—all so each of us can find Him, His love, and understand Him more. Like most of you, it was only when I lost everything that I found what I really and truly needed, which was a Savior, and then later when He became my Lord, then even later my Beloved. Can I deny anyone this same blessing? Doesn't a man need a relationship with Him too? Doesn't a man deserve to know the Lord personally? Is this only about what a wife needs or all about RMI and what we believe is it's ministry's goal? The truth is, RMI's goal has always been the same, which is to help each and every woman and man know the Lord personally.

Yes, God's desire is to restore, but not just marriages and families. It's restoring each of the individuals involved with Whom each person needs, Him only.

"The Lord turns the heart wherever He wishes . . ." (Proverbs 21:1) and this means our hearts, as women, can also be turned, by Him, too. So that husband's can also say, "You [God] have removed lover and friend far from me; my acquaintances are in darkness" (Psalm 88:18). Which means, if any person, a man included, doesn't turn to Him, then they too will say, "You [God] have removed my acquaintances far from me; You have made me an object of loathing to them; I am shut up and cannot go out" (Psalm 88:8).

The real danger is when a woman (or anyone) hardens their heart to what He is calling them to do. So as a minister, I must never interfere with what I see God doing in others and hope that in the process of Him taking me on this new journey, no one tries to interfere or judge me. I must never think for a millisecond that I know how His plan needs to be played out. "'For My thoughts are not your thoughts, neither are your ways My ways,' declares the Lord. 'For as the heavens are higher than the earth, so are My ways higher than your ways, and My thoughts than your thoughts'" (Isaiah 55:8–9). Instead, like Job, I will say, "I know that You can do all things, and that no purpose of Yours can be thwarted. Who is this that hides counsel without knowledge? Therefore I have declared that which I did not understand, things too wonderful for me, which I did not know. Hear, now, and I will speak; I will ask You, and You instruct me. I have heard of You by the hearing of the ear; but now my eye sees You; therefore I retract, and I repent in dust and ashes" (Job 42:1-6).

Chapter 7

Longing For Whom?

Therefore the LORD **longs** to be **gracious** to you,
And therefore He waits on high to have compassion on you
For the LORD is a God of justice;
How blessed are all those who long for Him.
—Isaiah 30:18

The key message to us in this opening verse is something I NEVER even noticed before. For over a year, every single day, I have read this verse but its true message had eluded me. It was not until I came to the place where I was able to say (and walk out in my life)—"**You** are all I need Jesus!" Its message? How *blessed* are those who LONG for Him!

Earlier on in this new journey, I had noticed that it says that He was *waiting* to have compassion, *waiting* to be gracious and even *waiting* to act, on our behalf, as a God of justice, but I never understood what He was *waiting* for—but now I know.

Our precious Bridegroom is *waiting* for us to also **long** and **yearn** for *only* Him! But instead, we long and yearn for someone or something else. We are unfaithful with our affections as our Beloved continues to allure us, to speak kindly to us, and does all that He can to remove the Baals (other gods we have put on an altar in our hearts) from our mouths and hearts. (Hosea 2:13–15).

In our society, the greatest god among women (from a young teen to an older woman) is their obsession with men. Young and old, never married, married, separated or divorced: women want and believe that they need and must have—a man in their life. The feminists chose their cure for this obsession by hating men and also trying to be like men, all so that they would not have this desire for a man nor be as vulnerable as women seem to be to men. This, however, did not solve the problem, because they did not go to the root or source of their dilemma.

Women were created to long and yearn for just One. It is when Eve sinned that she was cursed, "To the woman He said, 'I will greatly multiply your pain in childbirth, in pain you will bring forth children; yet your desire will be for your husband, and he will rule over you'" (Genesis 3:16). Not only did Jesus break the curse of sin ruling us, He broke every curse once we believed. As women we no longer need to suffer pain in childbirth (please read *Supernatural Childbirth* by Jackie Mize), nor do we need to long and yearn for a man, or any person who "doesn't have it" like we learned in the last chapter.

Instead, when we choose to turn our passion and thirst for the One who created us, and become His bride, then we will be filled with good things, all good things, since we are truly—His—His faithful bride. But sadly few women have reached this place of complete delight for Him. Instead, they chase after what they believe will bring them happiness. Remember in Psalm 37:4 it says, "Delight yourself in the Lord and He will give you the desires of your heart"?

Whether it is a young teenage girl who's missing her boyfriend or a wife who is separated from her husband (who has left her or she left him and now regrets it), there is an obsession of having a man that makes us, as women, especially vulnerable and prey to pain, rejection, suffering, loneliness, and the list goes on. The real tragedy is that the happiness that women believe will turn their lives around, which they believe is found in having a man, doesn't even exist.

We women, even though we are grown and no longer children, believe in fairy-tale romances. We read the stories as little girls and later as young women in romance novels. We watch make-believe couples in movies and on television, and even sing to songs about love. But these kinds of romances do not exist, any more than the stories of *Snow White* or *Cinderella* exist.

There is only *one* real love story and that is what is found in the Bible and in our Creator our Beloved.

God created every woman to yearn for the kind of love that we read about as little girls— but it can NEVER be filled with *human* love. The kind of love we need could only be fulfilled with His love, the agape and unconditional love that He proved for us at Calvary. Nothing else will satisfy us, let alone make our hearts soar.

Over the course of this year, while meeting many church missionaries and even RMI members who live in other parts of the world, I have seen that most women have tears or longing for their husbands, but even as believers, not that same longing for their Bridegroom. When women speak about their husbands, even the most professional and powerful women, they are immediately reduced to broken, tearful females who are falling apart. These women *long* for a person who actually loathes them! It is this sort of pathetic female that the feminist movement has gained such widespread appeal with today's women. This kind of yearning is nothing but tragic. To me, it's heartbreaking. Now there are young girls who choose to stay in abusive relationships after watching their mother do the same.

Yet the answer is not to leave a marriage with an abusive man, but to instead find a Lover. The Man who will protect her, which I have heard happens again and again because He is faithful! On the other hand, I do tell young girls I meet to never settle for a man who will not cherish them, when I am able to share my own testimony.

As believers, we need to turn away from the horrible obsession we have for men by turning our hearts and our passion for **more of His Love**, to the One who is able to heal our broken hearts. The women who have been rejected, "'For the Lord has called you, like a women forsaken and grieved in spirit, even like a wife of one's youth when she is rejected,' says your God," need to not only hear this lesson but see it in our own lives.

Only when we turn to Him will we say, "Let us rejoice and be glad and give the glory to Him, for the marriage of the Lamb has come and His bride has made herself ready" (Revelation 19:7). When we can all hear, "The Spirit and the bride say, 'Come!' And let the one who hears say, 'Come!' And let the one who is thirsty come; let the one who wishes take the water of life without cost," (Revelation 22:17) only then will we truly see what has been waiting and prepared for us who love Him.

When we, as believers, exhibit the kind of joy that He alone will give us, which follows from the commitment and faithfulness of wanting the Lord only, we will be capable of living a life and display a face that glows like a beacon in an ever darkening world. It is this kind of life that will draw every woman who is living in continuous and endless storms in their lives to want and yearn for what we possess, His love.

It is with unbelievable joy to see that many of us who discovered the ministry Erin founded, who are now able to focus on encouraging each other, move up even higher to this call, "for such a time as this" (Esther 4:14). Once passionate for restoration and in following the principles that lead to restoration, we are each now moving to this higher calling—only after becoming passionate for One only. Many women who find RMI confess they are no longer *seeking restoration*, but are instead *pursuing the Lord only!* And most women, at this point, result in being restored; yet some are not. And, I believe, some are not restored due them needing much more healing.

Just recently I read a praise report from someone who needed tremendous healing from her past of being molested as a child. Most people can never get over this, yet this brave woman became His lover and bride, and was even able to forgive her perpetrator. Had she not been left alone, even after losing custody of her own children, I am convinced, that she would never have found the healing she needed and deserved!

For those who are restored, and are like me, you may be called to lose your restored life in order to begin caring for the souls of the men in our lives who are also in need of our Savior. These men need to look to the Lord and have their needs filled by Him, because just as men cannot fill our needs as women, so too, we women can never fill a man's needs either.

"'If anyone wishes to come after Me, let him deny himself, and take up his cross, and follow Me. For whoever wishes to save his life shall

lose it; but whoever loses his life for My sake shall find it'"
(Matthew16:25).

Once we each become the Lord's bride, as His bride, we will radiate
this love for everyone to see.

Testimony

While in an airport just a couple of days ago, the lady at the counter
commented on my beautiful ring. Prior to my divorce, I had prayed
about a ring to wear so men would know I'm not available and I
eventually purchased a gorgeous ring that in the end, cost me nothing.
But this is an entirely different testimony that I hope to share later;
maybe later in the end of this book.

The lady at the airport counter asked me if I was a "newlywed"
because she looked down and saw the ring I was wearing was new. I
said, "Well, sort of," and I looked up and smiled. She then excitedly
said she could tell right away that I was "madly in love" because my
face just glowed! As I walked away, I felt as if my heart would burst
from the joy and love that overflowed for the Lord due to His
unlimited love He poured all over and through me. Then my mind
jumped to the realization of how most women look and feel after a
recent divorce—broken and aged, and again I wanted to share my
newly found Lover with them.

For several weeks before I left to tour the northeast of the U.S.A.,
being sent by my church (for what feels to me like the honeymoon
that I had only dreamed of), I had watched a series of shows on
television whose goal it was to help make a woman look ten years
younger. The show would always start out by showing pictures from
the woman's past (where she had once looked young and happy) and
then they would ask what had happened that had made her look the
way she looked now (downcast and old). Time and again, the woman
said that it was due to "a painful divorce." Each woman said that her
dreams had been shattered when things didn't turn out as she had
planned. Precious one—they never do!

Once again, God created us to need to be loved by One, and only One. And when we are unfaithful to Him, we end up with the very same broken life as if we were unfaithful in our earthly marriage and had become an adulteress. Things may seem fun and happy in the beginning, but later they always turn ugly—just as our marriage turned ugly because we longed for the wrong man. Then soon our countenance and appearance have also turned ugly, often due to bitterness rooted in unforgiveness, as we foolishly sought love from those who didn't and simply "don't have it."

Our pursuit, instead, needs to be for *more* of God and to become more intimate with our beloved Husband. To let Him be everything to us: Provider, Lover, Friend, Comforter, and Protector. It means moving from what we see, to the level of faith where we are living in the Spirit. For a woman who chooses this pursuit for her life, she will exchange her pain for joy and it will keep her immune to the ills, evils, and burdens of this world.

If Jesus died to give us an Abundant Life, then where is it, dear one? Certainly not in the lives of most Christian women today! And our lives, our compulsive desire for "our man" breeds this obsession in our daughters and the young women in our lives who are watching. We prove, through our tears and through our conversations (that ALWAYS center around the man whom we hope and pray will someday love us), that the goal in life is for a man, instead of the Son of Man. For women who have been rejected or abandoned by their husband, restoration and reconciliation are all that they can think and usually all they talk about, and this consumes every ounce of their energy.

Is it any wonder then why our Savior is still *waiting* on high to be gracious to us?

Dear reader, once you and I prove our love for our Beloved Bridegroom, then He will set the circumstances in our lives *right* to bless us in *all areas* of our lives: relationships (from your children to your siblings, parents, in-laws, husband and even in your workplace), finances (from always being short on funds to having even your heart's desires, not just your needs met), health (because with joy comes feeling good and no longer being susceptible to disease;

healing takes place in the spirit and in the body), and every other facet of our life.

No man in your life can do that! There is only One who has the power and resources to give us the Abundant Life as we truly become His beloved bride!

How did I let go of this obsession? It was simply getting more intimate with the One who was right there, alluring and speaking kindly to me—just as He is alluring and speaking kindly to you! There is no formula to intimacy. Just like everything else, it is just something you ASK Him for. For me, I simply told the Lord that I wanted to be closer, closer than any human who had walked the face of the earth…but I didn't know how, and I asked Him to do it. As a result of my simply asking, each day I continue to fall more and more in love with the Lover of my soul. I can see each day how He provides not just for my needs, but also for the desires of my heart!

Another example was also while traveling. I spent a few days up in Canada in a beautiful resort, all alone, with my Beloved. He brought me there to rest from traveling to several cities in just one week. There I witnessed firsthand that He expected nothing from me, nothing but my love for Him. I didn't spend my days reading my Bible or even praying. I didn't go there to fast (though at home, I have recently been fasting almost every day, eating just an evening meal). All I did was be there to rest in Him and in His awesome love. When I watched a romance movie on my computer, I kept thanking Him that I was no longer in deception (believing that what I was watching was real), but was instead, enthralled with the feeling that I could have and experience only with Him, just as every woman could!

Beloved, we need to encourage every woman to move beyond her pain and help her find peace, and then move from that peace to utter joy—all due to knowing and experiencing Him. It is more than possible for each and every one of you to experience the same thing, especially if you are currently hurting or have been rejected. This means that we simply change our focus from the man in our life to the Son of Man and Lover of our soul. And as we begin pursing Him, we will find that men will begin pursuing us! But I will never look back.

No man will ever win my heart again (only to break it and leave me wanting), not when there is One who laid down His life so I can live again!! Even a woman who is married must keep her heart for her Savior steadfast. This means her desires, and every secret of her heart, should be told to her heavenly Husband, not her earthly one.

One of my recent conversations with my ex-husband had him, once again, pursuing me for reconciliation. Both he and I were surprised when I asked him how he thought that he could compete with what I now have with the Lord! He had nothing to say, and in my heart, I could see how right what I said was. No man on earth can compete with what you will have when you gain the intimacy, love, and protection that your Bridegroom will give you when you truly *long* and *yearn* for Him. And when our longing is for the right One, then a husband will long for us, and continue to do so. It's not until a husband also longs for the only One who can fill his needs when he will experience peace and joy and the fulfillment most men lack.

This kind of love affair is a journey that begins with one step. All relationships are developed and grow based on the time and attention we give it. It may begin in reading your Bible, which are His love letters to you, or in singing love songs to Him. Though praise and worship songs are indeed wonderful, when you begin to move to love songs that foster intimacy, you are well on your way to a love affair that women will envy and will want to have too. There are many songs that are sung at Christian weddings that used to make my heart hurt; now these are the very songs that make my heart sing, knowing that I am loved and cherished for who I am by my Beloved.

Neither you nor I need to be any better or look any differently than we do—there is such freedom in knowing that! God created us just as we are and He cannot love us any more if we acted more in line with what a Christian ought to be. His love is the perfect love that casts out all fear. Then with that fear gone, it leaves more room for Him, and it will begin to show on your face.

Let's have no more tears for your (future, present or past) husband or ex or boyfriend, but let all your heart be for the One to whom you are betrothed as His beloved bride.

Let's put away the excitement for our earthly restoration, and focus on the relationship that we have right now with our true Husband— our Lord, Savior, and our Friend.

Let's have no more tears about love lost, but instead look to the future with Him. No longer in need of finding love or understanding, we can begin to live each day as the gift He has given to us.

For each of you who are hurting, fearful or lonely—you simply need more of His love. That's it. There is nothing else that will solve every problem in your life except more of Him.

Also if you have children, when they leave to visit their father, get excited because of how you'll be able to spend more time with Him. Then, you won't miss them anymore.

Testimony

When my children went to visit their father recently and to get to know the other woman more, I stopped myself from telling them that I would miss them. Instead I said, "Wow, you are going to have such a great time with Dad!" I told them that they never needed to worry about me, because they knew that I was always happy no matter where I was. And that because of the love we had for each other, they didn't need to miss me either, and simply needed to just have the best time with their dad since they had him all to themselves. Do you know how freeing this is for a child? Not to feel guilty for having a good time and not being burdened with how sad their mom is, all alone, at home?

You may wonder, too, if I worry about their exposure to their dads' lifestyle now or the other woman in my ex-husband's life (and her influence). The answer is "No." I know that God promises that everything will work together for my good and the good of my children! That's enough for me to not worry or give it another thought. If I believe His Word and His promise to me about salvation, then I can easily trust Him with everything in this life. And that leaves me to enjoy my life and live an abundant life.

Traveling for my church or as an ambassador for Erin's ministry, while being away from my children for extended periods of time, brings concern from many who question my sanity and even my love for my children. Being gone half of every month *is* extreme, to be sure, but again God promised that He would bring good from everything I do. Not just because I am being obedient to where He is calling me, but even if I did accidentally mess up— He promised to bless me!! With that kind of assurance, why would any of us choose to worry when we can instead be joyful? And it's also given my children ample time to be with their father who stays at our home while I am gone.

One bit of warning, be assured that the enemy will try his best to pour guilt all over your newly-found freedom with thoughts like: "You don't really care about your children anymore!" Just cast those thoughts down. Instead, it is simply that your priorities are now straight and God is rewarding you with no more pain or worry. You may even hear this same thing from friends, family and coworkers. Just resist going backwards (by entertaining these thoughts) and use that time and energy to move up higher.

After living this kind of life for only a few months, there is no way that I would ever take one step back. Instead, I have pledged my life to encouraging every woman in this world to say *yes* to God and to becoming the Lord's bride. It is my prayer that this chapter, and the rest of this book, will spark something inside of you that will fan the flames of passion for the One who is whispering—"Marry me."

Chapter 8

Who Are You Listening To?

For the time will come when
they will not endure sound doctrine;
but wanting to have their ears tickled,
they will accumulate for themselves teachers
in accordance to their own desires,
and will turn away their ears from the truth
and will **turn aside to myths**.
—2 Timothy 4:3–4

Just last night, I had one of the telephone calls that would normally have left me shaken for days or even weeks. My sister basically "lost it" when I got in the way of what she was desperate to do. The conversation ended with her yelling profane and unkind words into the phone before hanging up on me.

When it was over, I was amazed to find myself perfectly calm. Since she is my older sister, I could easily remember how this used to affect me. I have the personality that I long and work toward peace; I used to find peace at any cost. But my focus has changed from seeking peace with others to seeking peace with God and not worrying about what others say or trying to please them. My life with the Lord has been an incredible journey for me that has brought about incredible rewards. My desire in this chapter is to get you prepared to also take your own incredible journey with the Lord that goes well beyond freedom and leads, again, to your Abundant Life!

What kept me in peace when those words were hurled at me (and many others that preceded my sister's finale) was in knowing how my Lord and Husband felt about me. So that when any and all major situations arise such as this, going to Him immediately after (as I did the first time she called) or even right in the midst of the attack, I find peace. The Lord has taught me to ask Him what HE thinks of me or how HE feels about me, which I did when she hung up.

What HE said was vastly different than what I heard on the telephone. In addition to finding peace, I love how God actually has a sense of humor and His calmness, which most of us lack when we are in the midst of crisis. The Lord actually said, "Are you kidding?" when I asked Him if what she said was true. God also set up a "way of escape" by having someone call right in the midst of the first attack, which gave me time to ask my close friend to please pray (without sharing any details since this also comes with unwanted and unasked for advice). What was also part of God's plan so that I would **not** focus on the problem after she hung up; I instead needed to return my previous call, which resulted in my friend praying with me to bless my sister.

It used to be that I felt I "owed" it to my problem or to my enemy, to meditate on the problem and at least suffer through it a bit before releasing it! What nonsense. Now, due to being His bride, I keep all problems as far away from my heart and emotions as I am able to do as the Lord helps me. When insults or attacks are hurled at me, I separate myself emotionally and hide behind my Beloved and His love. So if you are experiencing an emotional attack right now, stop listening (and also by you repeating it over and over in your head) to what he or she said, and instead tune into what the Lord is saying to you.

If you are not at the place where you can hear God, hear the Lord speaking to you, then go to the Bible and read what He thinks of you. Keep reading until you find that peace that surpasses all understanding. And while searching, be sure to ask Him, "Is this what you think of me?" God will speak truth, but it will be up to you **who you will listen to**!

Most of us are more comfortable with knowing how to live and respond in unhappy or uncomfortable situations due only because we have done it more often. So, instead of letting a situation go, and meditating on how good God is and how much the Lord loves us, we choose to recount and replay unkind words. Much of what we learned came from our childhood and the lies we believed then, and sadly, *choose* to believe as adults rather than choosing to believe the truth. What is the truth? God is truth, His word is truth, and anything that doesn't line up with Him and His truth is nothing but a lie.

While on my last tour of meeting many of our church's missionaries and even RMI members who live in other parts of the world, I met women on the east coast and Canada, and I couldn't help but laugh by one comment that so many members expressed. Their first surprise at meeting me was how tall I am. But the second was that I was "so beautiful." The irony of this is that ALL of my life I was told by my family that I was NOT pretty, but instead was blessed with a good or outgoing personality. This never damaged me in anyway, but instead kept me focused on who I was on the inside rather than worrying about what I was told I was *not* on the outside.

When I married my FH, he was beside himself when he heard my family's opinion about my looks. One day, early in our marriage, I mentioned to my mother that he actually thought I was the prettiest of my sisters, to which she responded, "How sweet . . . love is so blind." Honestly, it must have been God all along who protected me from being scarred or damaged from these kinds of words, since I know that there are many of you who do suffer from what was said to you about your looks as a child. Though this did not do the damage as the enemy intended, what they said about my character did, probably since this is all that I thought I had. So when my sister attacked my character, it "had the potential" to really do harm.

One of our members told me (when I asked why she didn't smile for a picture we took that day) that her father told her never to smile, since she "looked stupid when she smiled." It was clear that she has never asked the Lord how HE felt about her beautiful smile, but instead has remained locked in a prison by believing a lie that was planted many years ago.

And reasoning or looking at the facts will never release you from what has been said to you in your past. No matter how many times my FH told me that I was pretty, coupled with the "fact" that for three years the Lord had my family (including ME) involved in a series of commercials, billboards, and brochures as (would you believe?) models, I never thought for a minute that I was pretty. It was only when my Beloved told me so that I believed that I was beautiful to HIM—since that is all that matters to me!

You may not be what our society believes is beautiful, but there is no doubt that is the way He feels about you! What society believes is pretty changes all the time, so why fixate ourselves and our feelings on something that changes— just as clothing styles change? It is not only foolish for us to get caught up in this menagerie of popular opinion, but it is also very dangerous since our daughters, and all the younger women in our lives will begin to do the same due to our example.

This does not mean that we are not to do anything to help us feel pretty. When we feel we look pretty, we act differently. That is why we need to go to God, again, and ask Him what He thinks of us. When we embrace the fact that God created us perfectly, then we will have the confidence to begin to dress and pamper ourselves accordingly. Yes, it can get way out of balance, especially if our looks are all we care about and concentrate on. But to neglect them is to try to fool ourselves into thinking we should never care about our outward appearance. If how we looked didn't matter, then God would not have told us how beautiful Sarah was (attracting a Pharaoh at her age still blows me away!) or Queen Esther, and how handsome David and Joseph were.

Some women are secure in their looks, but are instead plagued with other issues like being told they were stupid or uncoordinated or will always be fat because they are like their mother or grandmother who was overweight. None of this needs to keep you from the abundant life Jesus died to give you. You can free yourself from the prison that has you bound when you stop listening to the lies from your past (or present situation) and then begin, instead, to ask the Lord for HIS opinion. It is the truth that will set us free! So when our Husband tells us that we are beautiful or intelligent (because we have the mind of

Christ) then we must stop speaking the old lies and begin walking in faith with our newly found truth.

When we choose to believe a myth, which is defined as a falsehood, we keep ourselves from our abundant life. Our family, friends, or husband may have planted the lie, but when we continue to believe it, *we* are the one doing the watering that keeps the lie alive.

Remaining Quiet

There are also other dangers in listening to voices other than God's voice. We know from scripture that Saul lost his crown by listening to the voices of the people when they encouraged him to disobey God (read 1 Samuel 15:24). The young prophet lost even more by losing his life when he listened to the voice of the old prophet who invited him to dine with him instead of doing what God had told him (read 1 Kings 13:11-32).

Where would Jerusalem be if Nehemiah had succumbed to the mocking and had listened to the voices of the church leaders who wanted him to stop the rebuilding efforts of the walls and to come down to talk to them about it? (Read Nehemiah 6:1-9).

All of us need to learn to listen to and obey God's voice above anyone else's, including our own. This begins with our day-to-day living and not just for the important decisions we make. And what will continue complicating our ability of hearing and obeying God's voice are all the opinions that we are hearing from everyone around us, all because WE foolishly tell them what we are doing or about to do!

Let me confess that this has been the hardest lesson that I have yet to learn in my life! It seems almost daily that I foolishly share something in my life that I should have remained quiet about. We women love to share our lives with others, but I am not sure I am willing to suffer because of it any longer.

Recently, I have been hit with a major trial in my life dealing with my oldest sister who is about 14-years-old mentally but only about 4-

years-old emotionally, who is turning 65 this year. One of my other sisters had been her caregiver and called right before I left for a two-week tour insisting that I had to "take her." This is what instigated the hurled words I spoke of in the beginning of the chapter. However, I knew I couldn't have her here when I was traveling because I never told her that my husband had left again. It was in my ignorance and foolishness that I then shared the situation with some of my other siblings *after* I heard from God what I was to do. Are you surprised that what my siblings told me to do did not match up with what God told me to do?

This, then, created a current I had to swim against that made following God's plan much more difficult! Some of the difficulty stemmed from them questioning what I was planning to do next since all of the "suggestions" (that are normally, in my family, stated as orders) began to mingle with God's direction for what He wanted me to do.

The realization that I did not *have* to share my present situation of my recent divorce (and all the details that others expect for you to explain) came from the testimonies of RMI members who wisely remained quiet about their situations in their marriages (separation, their husband's adultery, and even their divorce). And due to them not sharing details of their lives, they were able to hear God more clearly and also to follow His lead without the confusion or opposition when family or well-meaning friends would have become involved. It also gave them time to deal with their own loss (of a husband or their marriage) and all the emotions that go along with it. Then later, when their family did "find out" they were able to deal with their family member's anger much more easily since they were stable (on the Rock).

Though I had followed this wisdom with my divorce this time, I continue to fail in other crises and just some of the day-to-day decisions that I face. It is clear that there is much more to a "gentle and *quiet* spirit" that I have yet to learn. When we "ponder things in our hearts" like Mary (the mother of Jesus) did, then our thoughts are all ours to seek God about and to be able to follow or deal with—with His help. We do not need to add to it other people's opinions or emotions that get in the way and often leave us confused, defeated, or simply tired.

It is my heart's desire to seek God more for this freedom as He gives me an even greater ability to remain silent and share things only with Him. This goes for giving more information than is necessary when speaking to people. In other words, I know that I need more discretion in my life. All of my recent problems, I know now, stem from my mouth and what I say. Very often, the area that we are the most anointed in, which in my life is my ability to speak, is also our greatest downfall; therefore, I personally need to turn it over totally to the leading of the Lord and the Holy Spirit.

Dear friend, whatever you are struggling with (your lack of discretion, your mouth, your emotions, or any other areas that you are dealing with), your Bridegroom wants to help you with it. He never wants you to struggle by carrying burdens that you have picked up or encumbrances someone has dumped on you. Instead, pass them to Him to carry for you. This will leave your arms open wide to embrace Him with the appreciation and love He deserves and is longing to receive from you!

Chapter 9

Give

Give, and it will be **given** to you.
They will pour into your lap a good measure—
pressed down, shaken together, and running over.
For by your standard of measure
it will be measured to you in return.
—Luke 6:38

For this particular chapter, unlike knowing what to call it didn't hit me immediately. Instead, I had so many titles I wanted to use. The message of giving is one that has been so abused, which ultimately led to its powerful principle being terribly neglected. The result of the abuse on giving, followed by the neglect of the message on giving, has caused the Christian community to no longer resemble "children of God"—instead we look like orphans.

Here are a couple of my titles:

Give—The Path Out of Poverty

Give When You Are in Need

As with every principle we have learned thus far, *giving* is totally the opposite of what comes naturally. When we are in need, *giving* is certainly the very last thing we feel like doing. I am no different than any of you. My flesh wants to control my life just like your flesh wants to control your life. Yet, as followers of the Lord (which being a Christian means), we are all striving to break out of our fleshly ways and live the abundant life, which means living by God's principles through the leading of the Holy Spirit and applying His grace to every difficult situation.

Being a follower means a dying to flesh and stepping out in faith, which is always unseen.

If you have seen all of Erin's video, you may remember her speaking of living "not by sight." And like me, you learned that God actually sets us up in a place of need in order to bless us. That it's at the juncture of our need when our fate, or blessing, stands before us, and it's we who choose. Our flesh wants to pull back, withhold, and look for another resource to fill the need in our life. However, as believers we are asked, instead, to walk by our faith even though we can't see what is up ahead. And it's our trust in the Lord that presses us forward.

For those who did not see the video, let me say that the Lord set me up in a very, very ominous position. Early one morning, I had gone into my online banking to print off the bank statement for my personal account and the church account. The balance took me by total surprise, as there was NOTHING left in either one. Over the course of the "hardest year of my life" many church members left after my husband's adultery was discovered: first, were the older members, then the men (who were also our largest donators), and later, the ones that remained, began experiencing financial hardship so they began not tithing or giving to the church. Let me pause here a moment and share this one principle that will literally change your life.

When you seem to have nothing left, you need to *give* in order to receive. If you fail to *give*, you will be left wanting.

"There is one who scatters, and yet increases all the more, and there is one who withholds what is justly due, and yet it results only in want. The generous man will be prosperous, and he who waters will himself be watered" (Proverbs 11:24–25).

The Message Bible puts it this way: "The world of the generous gets larger and larger; the world of the stingy gets smaller and smaller. The one who blesses others is abundantly blessed; those who help others are helped."

That morning, I was faced with utter ruin. For months, I had watched our church members update their personal profiles (that come into our office email) with "not giving" over and over and over again. On top of that, I had felt led (since it had been in my heart for YEARS) to *give* our prospective church members the required books to read for free online, rather than requiring them to purchase the books from our church bookstore. Then, due to this, our bookstore put these books on sale, and as a result, much of our church staff went to part-time since there no longer was enough work for full time employment.

If I wasn't living life in the fast lane (that feels more like the German Autobahn), I could have watched our finances spiral downward, but I had been too busy to really take time to notice—until that morning. That morning was like a splash of cold water in my face. The Lord told me months earlier about some of these changes, but it was back when financially I was more than fine. God had purposely waited until I could see clearly that I was about to go under to ask me to give.

"So when He heard that he [Lazarus] was sick, He then stayed two days longer in the place where He was . . . So when Jesus came, He found that he had already been in the tomb four days" (John 11:6, 17).

The Lord had set me up for a huge blessing and so that His Father would be glorified. But for that to happen, He had to lead me to that one gate, which is narrow and hard to find. *"Enter through the narrow gate; for the gate is wide and the way is broad that leads to destruction, and there are many who enter through it. For the gate is small and the way is narrow that leads to life, and there are few who find it" (Matthew 7:13–14).*

The Lord spoke to me that morning, just after seeing I had nothing left, that He wanted me to go into our online church store and discount all of our books, videos and audiotapes, but it didn't end there. When that was complete, He told me to go in and set our church member discount code to 50% off, up from the 20% that we had been giving to our church members for years. The result would be us having no profit at all. The price would just cover our cost to print.

Looking at the facts, this move would lead to our church collapsing, but what options did I really have? The Lord had taught me over the years to trust in Him and Him alone. No longer did works or devising a different plan enter my mind, and really I was in much too deep not to try something so stupid. On top of that, God had put in my heart a passion to *give*, which stemmed directly (or should I say "flowed directly") from His heart of *giving* to mine.

Over the course of the previous year, I had been *given* so much from the Lord: love, compassion, comfort, security, peace, joy, patience, goodness, and the list goes on and on. As a result, all I wanted to do was *give*: *give* of my time, *give* of my overflow of love, *give away* everything that had been *given* so freely to me! There had been so many times when I found myself at the end of all my resources, only to be put in a place where God asked me to *give* out of my lack, and when I did—I was again overflowing!

Let me share just a couple of examples that don't include financial giving so that you can see that giving when you are in need is a principle to follow, not a law that we must obey or feel oppressed under.

The first one the Lord brought to mind was on my first, very long, meeting our church members' tour. I was exactly half way through (flying to 14 cities in 16 days) and I was exhausted! I had no idea how I was going to make it. So I retreated to my room to talk to the Lord about it. While at my lowest, the Lord prompted me to go downstairs and to bless my precious hostess with a hair and makeup "make-over." When I wanted to withdraw, the "opportunity" came for ME to *give*.

That night I didn't get to bed early as is my normal routine, but let me tell you that when I woke up, I had more energy and enthusiasm than I did when I began my trip! Instead of withholding, I *gave* out of the tiny bit of energy I had left and the result was nothing short of miraculous.

The next opportunity that came to mind was again when I came to the end of myself (and my strength). It occurred a few months after my divorce when being "a single mom" again was taking its toll. I had just taken over my FHs position in our church (other than preaching), so that our income as pastors would continue. So on top of my own position with our church, which was ministering to thousands of women, I had to take over all his other duties at the church and also around our house. In addition, I had begun traveling two weeks out of every month to help recover from the adultery scandal when we lost many of our television audience and members. In addition, my children were still struggling with their own loss, so when I was home, I needed to take it on myself (relying on God's strength of course), by taking over many of the chores my children used to do for me such as all the cooking.

That day my strength seemed to run out. I was just sitting at my FHs desk in our home office wondering how I was going to make it, when God brought in the "opportunity" to overcome my exhaustion by *giving* so He could bless me.

First, an email came in from my brother who lives oversees. He wrote to tell me that he had "gone ahead and booked a flight for my niece" (who was 16 years old) to come to live with us for a year. I just sat there stunned (because I had written to him that she could NOT come, then later found out that I had actually sent it to the wrong email address). A moment later in walks my son who tells me that his friend was just kicked out of his house and asked if he could come live with us. Not only was it just another body in our home—this boy was huge and could really eat!

Not ten minutes later, my daughter came in to ask me what she should do. It seemed that her friend had been locked out of her house, her mom was at a weeklong conference, and she didn't know how to help her.

At this point, our flesh wants to scream and run, but deep in our spirits, if we find that quietness in our hearts, we can faintly hear the Lord alluring us with His love, asking us to *give*. The abundance of His love has "set us up" in order to bless others, not to keep it for ourselves.

- It is not until we are backed up against the Red Sea that the waters will part for us to walk through (not to mention our enemies being drowned).

- It is not until there is no wine at the wedding feast that the first miracle in our lives will be performed.

- It is not until we have our last meal with our only child that a prophet will come along and ask us to bake him a cake, so that our kitchen will be filled with oil to pay off our debts and make us prosperous (read 1 Kings 17:8-16). Instead our flesh wants to eat to feed that cake to our own child who is starving and about to die.

Since I knew God and knew His principles, and also knew the Lord's endless love for me, without the least inclination that it would lead to an abundance of strength, I gladly agreed to have my niece come to live with us, also the young man moved in downstairs with my boys, and so did my daughter's friend, who shared their room upstairs. The result was finding unlimited energy that had been super charged by the Holy Spirit! I was able to take on more than I had before, and instead of struggling with the "poor me, what am I going to do" syndrome, I was able to fight against it with ease. Rather than struggling as I had just been feeling, I was gliding through everything with unlimited energy, joy in my heart, and praise on my lips. All I could see now was God's hand and His provisions surrounding me, not the lack that was once looming over me.

And ladies, it didn't stop with physical abundance. Abundance is also where I am now financially, not impoverished like I was that morning when I looked at our bank balance. Just minutes after I obeyed and opened my home to 3 young people, the opportunity to get out of debt literally came to my door. The "lack" in our bank accounts ended in the most incredible blessing that I have ever seen, but not before the Lord showed me another place I needed to give out of my lack.

Later that very same day, as I said, I had nothing in either of the bank accounts. The Lord had me go pick up a book order for our church library, which were mostly new bibles. Immediately after the young man loaded all the boxes into my car, the Lord spoke to me that He wanted me to *give* away everything, not charging anything, not even recovering our cost. Instead, He wanted me to sow these into the lives of the homeless in local shelters, and He laid out the entire plan as I was driving back to the church. All of these "opportunities" were leading me to fulfilling my huge financial need, but not before God allowed the final "opportunity" for me to *give*. The result was instantaneous—that very evening I opened my computer and a huge donation came in by email, which was the largest single donation our church had ever received!!

Had I not obeyed each and every "opportunity" that the Lord presented to me, I would not have been **open** to receive the huge blessing I and our church received that day. Here is the principle to abundance:

The bigger the crisis of need will require the larger obedience, which results in the greater the blessing that overflows—*pressed down, shaken together, and running over.*

Therefore, if your arms are burdened, carrying incidentals that belong to others, when He asks you to give—your arms will not be open to receive what He plans to give you.

So many women want to have blessings like this in their lives, but are unwilling to *give* the tiniest thing they have in order to receive. Just begin to *give* what you have when you see that the Lord has *given* you the opportunity to do so.

One key principle that we must keep in the back of our minds, but not to the point that it will imprison us to be afraid to walk boldly with the Lord in the area of *giving*, is that the enemy, the devil, also loves to disguise himself to get us off track. How many times have I seen women literally "throw themselves off a cliff" only to find themselves in a mess for everyone to witness as a mocking to their "faith"? God does not ask us to do crazy things (remember the enemy has a voice too), though to some everything we do seems crazy. So how do we know the difference?

Of course, knowing God's voice is key, and that happens just being in His presence and letting Him speak to you every morning and throughout the day. This is different than reading the Bible—but reading His Word is where you must start. Knowing His principles will also keep you from going astray because His Word gives you wisdom and lets you know what He might call you to do, and what He would tell you to do. Lastly, it is just sitting still and listening for that still small voice, so that you can recognize His voice over all the rest.

This also includes not asking for or listening to everyone's opinion about what you should do. Even if you don't "ask" for advice, you are going to get advice if you tell everyone (or even just a few or sometimes just one person) what is happening in your life. This is when that "gentle and QUIET spirit" needs to be put into action. Be quiet about what is going on in your life and instead talk to the Lord—turn off your phone so you know His voice above anyone else's.

Secondly, I have found that the enemy loves to get me off track by feeding my "self-righteous flesh." He loves to puff me up so that I can imagine the great testimony I will be able to share if I do this or that! If this is your motivation, then it means you are instead throwing yourself off a cliff only to make a fool of yourself when things turn out badly.

Another wrong motive is when some women do the outrageous in order to show someone, other than the Lord, how much they care or are willing to do to prove their love—especially husbands or FH. If this is your motivation, then you are still in idolatry by putting your husband (or someone else and their opinion or their love) above the Lord's.

For the most part, doing what God is calling you to do will mean 1) walking out one of God's principles, like giving, 2) will be something that no one will praise you for, 3) and will be a testimony that you would rather *not* share with most people you know because they "wouldn't understand" and probably think you've gone nuts.

Here is another destructive motivation: "If I give $$$ to RMI my marriage will be restored." Precious one, God doesn't take bribes and RMI has never asked me or you for money. Usually when the Lord is calling you to *give* (or obey in another way) you don't have a particular reward in mind. You are simply determined to *give* when asked or to obey when told.

Let me close with a few more testimonies, since God said that we would be able to overcome the wicked one by His precious blood AND by the word of our testimony (read Revelation 12:11).

The first real big financial test for me happened *immediately* after my divorce when I, for the first time in 16 years, was in charge of our family's finances. My husband left me all of our debt and was adamant that he would not be paying child support either. When I looked at ALL the bills, I was overwhelmed. So I went to the Lord to ask Him where I was to begin. He immediately brought to mind our church's building pledge. We, as a couple, had pledged $10,000 to be paid over two years; yet there was less than two months left and $7,000 remained to be paid. The Lord said He wanted me to start there.

Remember how I said I still have a way to go to not share what I am doing or about to do with others? Well I cannot tell you how many people tried to stop me from doing what, really, I could not do without God's help. So I tried to explain I simply did not have that kind of money. But I knew that as I walked forward with the right heart, He would make a way if this *was* His plan. Amazingly God showed me the way and just **two hours** after I put that $7,000 dollar check in the offering, I received $10,000 dollars (the entire pledge) back!

My opening testimony, when I had nothing in our bank accounts, later led to an incredible refinancing option that would mean no debt other than a house payment (even my car was about to be paid off) and another check that a television member wrote to tell me was coming for my women's ministry that was almost $15,000.

Remember, this happened only after I saw, that same morning, for me to pay the bills I could *see* would mean being overdrawn. I *saw* day-after-day the "not giving" updates from the members' profiles, as I *saw* the drop in online book and video sales, but in comparison to the promises of God, asking me to trust Him, I was able to obey each time He asked me to give, even when I lacked, which enabled me to grow strong in faith and in the end, giving glory to God!

"Without becoming weak in faith he contemplated his own body, now as good as dead since he was about a hundred years old, and the deadness of Sarah's womb; yet, with respect to the promise of God, he did not waver in unbelief but grew strong in faith, giving glory to God, and being fully assured that what God had promised, He was able also to perform" (Romans 4:19–21).

Let me close by stating I deserve no pat on the back "oh ye of little faith," but with the faith of a mustard seed I *saw* that mountain of financial lack plummeting into the sea.

Dear reader, sow that mustard seed of faith as the Lord leads you and watch for those "opportunities" to *give* when you are faced with a "lack" knowing that, precious one, God is about to open the Red Sea behind you—so pack your bags because you are about to walk *through* on dry land while the waters engulf and drown your enemies!

Chapter 10

Surrender

He who has found his life will lose it,
and he who has lost his life for My sake will find it.
—Matthew 10:39

Surrender is the path to the abundant life, and therefore it is something that we struggle with. Surrender simply means to give up control of and to place our destiny in the hands of another. However, as long as we maintain any control over any aspect of our lives, we lose the opportunity for real freedom, the freedom that brings both joy and peace.

The very first time that we surrender our "lives" to the Lord and accept His plan of salvation, we take the first step. All of us can remember the freedom and joy that meant: feeling clean, forgiven, and for the first time, our future looked bright. But God is not satisfied (thank you, Jesus) to leave us there. He tells us that He wants to bring us from glory to glory (2 Corinthians 3:18).

As we move from glory to glory, His Holy Spirit will slowly begin showing us different areas of our lives that need to be refined. Ultimately, He will ask us to surrender that thing (or person) in our lives to His loving hands—HIS plan for our lives or "*Thy* will be done." It normally begins with a trial or feelings that overwhelm us: we simply can't do it or face it any more. It is then that either we *try* to make just "one more plan" or we recognize that we are again in a place of surrender.

"Abide in Me, and I in you. As the branch cannot bear fruit of itself unless it abides in the vine, so neither can you unless you abide in Me" (John 15:4).

The Lord has brought me through surrendering so many things and people in my life that a person would think that there could be no more left to give over to our Savior. But I believe now (at the ripe age of 50 years) that our lists are each endless, and that you and I will never get to the bottom of the barrel.

For instance, after I reached my forties, with the birth of my last child, I found I had a weight problem. Diets that had always worked in the past no longer touched the "baby fat" that remained after her birth. To complicate matters, my family has a history of thyroid problems. Most of my siblings are on lifelong medication and yet, they still battle weight, sleepiness, cold hands and feet, all of which were signs that were screaming at me after my last birth, but it was the body in my mirror that got my attention.

God was not about to let me carry the burden, "For My yoke is easy and My burden is light" (Matthew 11:30). So, instead, He graciously began to "pile the burdens" until they were too much for me to carry. One day I cried out to the Lord and simply gave my weight issues to Him. From that moment on (to this very day) I never weighed myself or watched what I ate again, nor did I seek medical help for my thyroid symptoms as my siblings had been pushing me to do.

Of course, if the Lord had led me on this path to seek help, I would have obeyed. It is not wrong to seek help from doctors as King Asa did: *"In the thirty-ninth year of his reign Asa became diseased in his feet. His disease was severe, yet even in his disease he did not seek the LORD, but the physicians"* (2 Chronicles 16:12). However, God just wants us to go to HIM first and then **He** will lead us on the path to health, whether it be through doctors or some other way. My own beliefs is that it depends on your particular journey and where you are in regard to your faith.

What's interesting is, our toughest challenge is NOT the initial surrender, but the following three to four months when we are so tempted to do "something." If it is your weight that you have surrendered, you will keep thinking that you *should* "at least" cut back on what you are eating, or drink more water, or add more fruits or vegetables to your menu. Maybe exercise should be important to faithfully do. But if you simply resist each temptation, very soon the Holy Spirit will take over. And during the wait, spend more and more time with the Lord and each time you think of it, keep surrendering it to Him. And do yourself a favor, resist the temptation to help God out—I've been there and done that, and it doesn't work.

The result of surrendering my weight was to never have to diet again. God keeps me at the weight I should be and He doesn't stop there. My children, especially my daughters, are thrilled that He also keeps me in the current clothing trend to show His glory, not my willpower. The glory of it all in my life is that I can use the time I would normally use thinking and concentrating on dieting (what I should eat, counting calories or carbohydrates, weighing myself, vigorously exercising etc. etc.), to seeking more of the Lord and being free to spend more time thinking of Him! Here is my favorite verse I recited in my head and heart that I clung to:

*". . . do **not** be worried about your life, as to what you will eat or what you will drink; nor for your body, as to what you will put on. Is not life more than food, and the body more than clothing? But seek first His kingdom and His righteousness, and all these things will be added to you" (Matthew 6:25, 33).*

Then, just last year, when I was given our finances and all the debt to go with it in the divorce (as I've mentioned in many previous chapters), immediately I was overwhelmed, so I simply passed my burden onto my Beloved Husband. However, as He began to dig me out and give me the wisdom and knowledge that I lacked, I found myself beginning to reason and plan—only to feel just as overwhelmed and fearful as before. Once again, and again and again, I had to surrender and acknowledge that: "apart from Him I can do nothing" (John 1:3)! The result was that peace and joy again followed each time I surrendered this area of my life, and my only job remained to resist planning or thinking about it.

"Trust in the Lord with all your heart and do not lean on your own understanding. In all your ways acknowledge Him, and He will make your paths straight" (Proverbs 3:5–6).

The truth is—thinking and reasoning will ultimately lead to worry and fear, which takes time and energy away from intimacy with the Lord. He has told me time and again that He does not need a wife or a helper—He is complete. What He longs for is a **bride** who is not stressed and consumed with problems.

What, of the many things, I love about the Lord is that He has graciously and lovingly given too many burdens—all at the same time over the past year, just so that I would give all of it to Him and enjoy a full year that feels just like a dream-come-true honeymoon. Many, who really don't know or understand or can unfathomable the love He has for us, reason that when something awful happens, or too many things happen at once, that somehow God is punishing them or is not there for them—especially when things start to overwhelm them, and they can see no way out. But that is so far from the truth! The truth is that He loves us so much that He doesn't want us to struggle or carry even one tiny thing that will weigh us down with burdens or cares. He knows that until it is simply too difficult to carry, we won't lay it down at His feet.

As I was preparing and pondering this chapter, I realized I had become so overwhelmed with so many areas of my life that I had no idea I was still trying to hold together and to make happen by myself. Please understand that in every area of my life, I have sought God for help, but the moment my restored marriage collapsed with the announcement that my husband was filing for divorce, I realized that I had (for years) tried to fulfill what I had always wanted in my life. I had always wanted to simply be a good wife, a stay-at-home mother who homeschooled her children, and to simply be a keeper of our home. The honest truth is that I was so happy and content to be at home, that when I didn't leave the house for over a week, I was actually the happiest.

Then one day my life changed in an instant. I had no choice, really, other than to seek the Lord wholly and to surrender my future for His. In an instant, I was traveling, which I was terrified to do as I don't like meeting new people or strange surroundings. In an instant I was the breadwinner and provider of my very large family, and instantly, I became a pastor and administrator of a megachurch and worldwide television ministry. But by looking up, into the face of my Beloved, I was able to "do it all" and to do it easily, only because I surrendered it totally to Him. Instead of my having to try, it was His strength, His wisdom, powered by His love that accomplished it all.

It's now nine months later since it all happened, and I have been asked to face another area of my life that I hold dear: homeschooling—what to do about my youngest children's education. Due to all my traveling, which is not an option (if I remain in my husband's former and my current position with the church), coupled with the opportunities that have opened up for my older children so that they can't help me at home any longer, my younger children are often working on their schooling alone. This does have its benefits, but without following up and at least some guidance, I can see that they are not getting the education that they deserve. It became clear just weeks ago that I had to surrender this area of my life to Him, but not before the enemy began screaming in my ear, "what people would think if I put my children in public school!" Then he reminded me about "the shame I just went through when everyone found out about the divorce. Surely this proved that public school is where my children are headed" the enemy persisted.

The truth is, God isn't saying anything of the sort. He simply wants to free me up and has asked me to surrender another area of my life— reminding me of how hard I had *tried* to be a perfect wife only to see my marriage end. The same people who, like Job's friends, thought or told me that I must have failed to follow *A Wise Woman* principles would certainly have a hay-day when they found out that my children started going to public school.

However, there it was, that still, small voice who reminded me of how He had brought me through that very difficult and devastating period of my recent divorce and how much JOY I had, sheer joy I never dreamt would be possible. He reminded me that this joy came as I moved toward my fear rather than pulling back, and that my reputation was again in His hands.

Looking back to when I first began to travel, I wanted so much to pull back and to hide; but instead, I moved toward my fear, and that's when the chains that had me bound began to fall off. They didn't fall off all at once, but as I surrendered rather than trying to overcome, one-by-one, they fell off. The Bible says that we are overcomers, but it is not because we have the ability in ourselves to overcome. Instead, it is the Lord who makes us overcomers as we put our trust in Him.

*"For whatever is born of God **overcomes** the world; and this is the victory that has overcome the world—our faith" (1 John 5:4).*

Finances, too, have come to overwhelm me and to cause me to fear. But as I have moved toward the fear, and chosen to GIVE when He provided the opportunity, the Lord has faithfully begun to take over, and I know that I will be out of debt supernaturally soon.

Today I am at a place in my life (finally) that I am convinced (because of the proof of His love in my life) that everything He calls me to do or to go through ultimately will lead to freedom and blessings! All I need to do is to wait for Him to show Himself.

Yet, let me be perfectly transparent. A day does not go by that I don't think that I need to make some kind of a plan to give my children a better education now or wonder how I can help budget, calculate, or chart how to get out of the financial mess that I am in. But praise the Lord, I am resisting so that I am leaving room for God to show His glory. I just need to be still (in mind, body and spirit) and to know that He is God.

Dear reader, no matter what area of your life you are now struggling with, instead of holding on, surrender it to the Lord. Don't use your strength or any other natural abilities to handle it or fix it (and for heaven's sake, don't seek outside help). Instead, realize how true this passage is and meditate on it.

*"I am the true vine, and My Father is the vinedresser. Every branch in Me that does not bear fruit, He takes away; and every branch that bears fruit, **He prunes it so that it may bear more fruit** . . . Abide in Me, and I in you. As the branch cannot bear fruit of itself unless it abides in the vine, so neither can you unless you abide in Me. I am the vine, you are the branches; he who abides in Me and I in him, he*

bears much fruit, for apart from Me you can do nothing" (John 15: 1–5).

Surrender whatever it is that has overwhelmed you to the Lord today, this very minute, so that He can give you more of an abundant life than you ever dreamed existed.

──────── Chapter 11 ────────

Je t'aime Maman

I have **no greater joy** than this,
to hear of my children walking in the truth.
—3 John 1:4

In the last chapter "Surrender," I left off with surrendering so many
new areas of my life to the Lord. One that was of deep concern to me
(before I turned it over to the Lord) was my younger children's
education.

As with all areas that I have turned over to His finished work, there is
always a period of waiting that is required before He begins to move.
This is a time of testing and resting—and of trust. While waiting, the
enemy (or maybe it is simply our flesh) will tempt us to do
"something!" If we are trusting the Lord for our weight loss, we will
be tempted to "at least" drink more water, stop eating sweets, or take
smaller portions. But we must resist that temptation and make sure we
tell the Lord that we are helpless and hopeless without Him taking
care of this area of our lives.

It was the same way while I waited on the Lord to move in the area of
schooling my children. I was willing to send them to school: private
or even public (something I had spoken so adamantly against). Yet,
surrender means giving up our will for His will, which means the
enemy will be doing what he can to get in the way of what the Lord
has planned for us. So once I fully surrendered the enemy began
trying to persuade me with thoughts (remember our battle is often
won or lost in our minds) that the Lord, whom I was trusting in, had
made me go through a scandalous divorce, and so—sending my
children to public school was certainly next on His list.

However, as I praised Him for even that possibility, knowing, too, that though scandalous and high profile, my divorce has brought immeasurable blessings beyond what anyone could hope or think was possible! That was when the Lord spoke to me that just as He had blessed my baby sister (who is somewhat "intellectually and emotionally challenged" to move close by, so I could help with her care just a few months earlier), in the same way, He assured me that He would bless my children with something wonderful, something I never thought of! So I shared this with my younger children and they were relieved and full of faith believing with me as we waited.

It was only three days before I left for a European tour (leaving my children for three weeks without any clue as to how they would manage their schooling while I was gone), that the Lord began to move!!! My sister, who as I said is challenged, has many amazing gifts. And so I'd know this was His plan, when I told my sister that I was on my way to Paris (as one of my destinations), she began speaking little phrases in French to me. A few days later it clicked, and I asked if she would be interested in tutoring the children in "a little French." Then the Lord reminded me that she had also lived for a couple of years with a family from Mexico and that she could speak conversational Spanish really well. I asked if she would also teach them Spanish when she ran out of things that she knew in French.

My sister was so excited and replied that she would love to tutor them, but that her real love was spelling! That's when I remembered that she had an incredible gift for spelling! So I hired her to tutor them in all three subjects! This revelation led me to follow His lead and I asked my niece (who came to live with us for a year), and who is excellent in mathematics, to tutor the children when she came home from school. My niece was so honored and she agreed immediately, telling her cousins and her parents how important it made her feel. This led me then to ask my oldest son (who is an excellent writer) to tutor the children in their written reports (science, history, and geography). Lastly I asked my special needs son to help the children in reading and to help hone their skills as an orator (reading or speaking aloud) since he feels inadequate in these subjects. So tutoring others will also help him as he helps his younger siblings! Within just one day (and just three days before I left), the Lord (not I) pulled this all together!!

The results were amazing. The first time that I was able to speak to my children with a chat while in Europe, in my hotel room in Belfast, Ireland, just as we said our good-byes, my son came close to the camera and whispered, "Je t'aime Maman, Je t'aime" (pronounced za *tem* ma'ma). It means, "I love you mother, I love you"! Ladies, all I could do was cry! How precious is our dear, sweet Husband—my goodness, we simply can never really fathom His care for us! Oh the heights and depths of His love!!!

Letting Go

With this testimony now shared, let me speak to you, dear reader about your failure to let go of your marriage restoration, or of finding a husband (for those who are not yet married), or of a good marriage (for those of you who are still married but who are miserable). Erin often shares of how she longs to be able to help each of you more, so I'd like to help her since she's helped me so much.

If I was convinced that God would certainly allow me to continue to homeschool my children, and if I had held onto (not letting go) of the real possibility of sending my children to public school, then I would never have left room, nor would my heart be right with trusting God. Therefore, He would never have been able to work in this area of my life. So, too, are you who refuse to let go of the "promise" that the Lord may have given you in regard to your marriage (present, past, or future marriage).

The Lord gave me those same promises too. However, as my intimacy with Him grew, so too did my desire for Him alone. And at that point, nothing else mattered, and all the promises that He gave me, I gave them back to Him. What He gave me, as a replacement, was the Abundant Life that I am living now. The way I am living now is what I was created to do. It was nothing that I may have wanted or planned, but as we all know, His ways and His thoughts are far above our thoughts and plans!!!

"The mind of man plans his way but the Lord directs his steps" (Proverbs 16:9).

"'For I know the plans that I have for you,' declares the LORD, 'plans for welfare and not for calamity to give you a future and a hope'" (Jeremiah 29:11).

"This is God's Word on the subject: "I'll show up and take care of you as I promised and bring you back home. I know what I'm doing. I have it all planned out—plans to take care of you, not abandon you, plans to give you the future you hope for" (Jeremiah 29:11 Message).

"'For My thoughts are not your thoughts, neither are your ways My ways,' declares the Lord. 'For as the heavens are higher than the earth, so are My ways higher than your ways, and My thoughts than your thoughts'" (Isaiah 55:8–9).

Had I held onto my marriage restoration "promise" (Hey, Lord, you promised!!), for instance, not only would I not have this life, but I would also have continued to experience pain, after pain, after pain! Erin continues to see this kind of pain in praise reports and I've even read far too much pain in other things written by some of RMI's leaders—pain that is accepted as normal when it simply is not His plan! And I've spoken to Erin about it because I know it grieves her too.

Once all of the heart ties are severed (for every need on this earth: physical, material, and emotional), and the promise has been put on the altar (each and every promise), that's the moment that you will begin to experience "no more tears and no more sorrows." Let me give you an example.

When I heard that my former husband had a wedding date set, it did not hurt, not one bit. Instead, I honestly rejoiced, knowing that my future with my precious Husband was more secure than ever!! When I heard that all of my children had finally come to the place where they would not only *attend* their father's wedding, but would actually be *in his wedding with the AW*, it too was a time to rejoice because I could see that they were following my lead in trusting God in areas that most children (and adults) find impossible. "I have **no greater joy** than this, to hear of my children walking in the truth" (3 John 1:4).

Dear reader, surrender means freedom from worry, pain, confusion, and loneliness. It is a place of *rest* while you watch miracles happen right before your eyes. It sets you free so that you can spend more time and enjoy greater intimacy with the Lord, which is what He wants from us! He longs to spend time with us, not discussing our needs and troubles, no more than that kind of discussion would foster intimacy in a marriage between a husband and a wife!

Without truly surrendering, however, you will never experience true joy and the freedom that the Lord died to give you! What a tragedy*!! It is just as heartbreaking as those who never accept His death to free them from hell and eternal damnation.* But it may be even more heartbreaking for our precious Savior who is on bended knee asking you to be His bride. How He longs for each of your hearts, but your heart (your thoughts, what you talk about, what you dream about, and what you write about) is all about your earthly husband or boyfriend. Can you really compare the two? Is someone you can see so necessary when there is One who is unseen Who can meet and exceed all the dreams you have ever had over your entire lifetime—and more that are so far above that you've never even dreamed them?

"For from days of old they have not heard or perceived by ear, nor has the eye seen a God besides You, Who acts in behalf of the one who waits for Him" (Isaiah 64:4).

"God can do anything, you know—far more than you could ever imagine or guess or request in your wildest dreams!" (Ephesians 3:20 Message).

Just two nights ago, I spoke to the Lord regarding continuing to help with RMI as I had been doing after reading some of the praise reports and columns that were submitted, but hadn't yet been posted on the website. It was clear that most of RMI members still want their marriage restored above all else (and the young women want an earthly husband, not a Heavenly one). It seems that this topic is screaming at me in every column and praise report. And if so, who am I to help in leadership when I honestly really don't want restoration myself? Yes, that's a true statement. I have been fully restored to my Husband after waiting a lifetime for Him, and now I see He is more than I could have imagined a Husband could be! So why would I want to settle?

So each time I interact with a RMI member, who oozes excitement in her voice and dreaminess in her glazed over eyes, and she asks me if I believe that my marriage will be restored again, my heart is pierced. What I want to ask is, if God gives us the desires of our hearts and your heart is for God to restore *my* marriage, what about my heart and my desires? My heart is for my Heavenly Husband, my Beloved! "So who am I Lord," I ask, "to remain helping Erin and be a leader over this body of believers (who want their marriage restored or to capture a Christian husband)?"

That's when the Lord reminded me of this verse that I have read nearly every day for about ten years. It was only a few months ago when I finally understood what it meant:

"And if you extract the **precious** from the **worthless**, *You* will become My spokesman . . ." (Jeremiah 15:19).

"The precious," that this verse refers to, dear one, is the Lord— meaning everything else is worthless! That means your marriage restoration (or finding a Christian husband), money, reputation, children, position, career, etc. Everything but Him is worthless.

This means for those of you who are angry with me or disappointed in me, or even judge that I lack as a leader and am disqualified to help Erin, remember that it was Jesus who told us, "He who loves father or mother more than Me is not worthy of Me; and he who loves son or daughter more than Me is not worthy of Me" (Matthew 10:37).

The Lord told me that when I, too, shared the same "passion" and "obsession" for marriage restoration as I am seeing in the RMI ministry, it was then I wasn't fit to be His spokesperson. But now that I have finally seen the light, just as Erin has seen it too, knowing just Who He really is and what He wants to be in my life (and in yours), I finally became His spokesperson and that's when I began traveling all over the world!

Yes, these are hard words for many people to accept, so I am prepared to see many walk away from RMI, judge Erin and shun me.

"Looking at him, Jesus felt a love for him and said to him, 'One thing you lack: go and sell all you possess and give to the poor, and you will have **treasure in heaven**; and come, follow Me.' But at these words he was saddened, and **he went away grieving**, for he was one who owned much property" (Mark 10:21–22).

Better than the riches of this world,
Better than the sound of my friend's voices,
Better than the biggest dreams of my heart,
And that's just the start!

Better than getting what I say I need,
Better than living the life that I want to,
Better than the love anyone could give—
Your love is!

You hold me now in your arms and never let me go . . .

I can't stop falling in love with You!
I'll never stop falling in love with you!!!

I can't stop falling in love with You!
I'll never stop falling in love with you!!!

Chapter 12

Your Best Protection

O LORD, You **surround** [me] with **favor** as with a shield.
—Psalm 5:12

It seems as if at least once a day I find myself trying to find safety: to protect myself, whether emotionally, physically, financially or in any other way.

Trying to find protection also spills over to wanting to protect my children. What mother doesn't try to protect her children? Yet I have found, when backed into a corner, *my* protection (for myself and also for my children) is basically no protection at all.

If you have lived in an abusive situation, you know how your life is riddled with schemes of finding safety and protection. Whether that abuse is verbal, emotional, physical or sexual, you try one way after another to try to stop whatever or whoever is coming against you (and/or your children).

It wasn't until someone really confronted me about my beliefs about abuse, and abuse of the worst kind for a mother (when a father is abusing his own child), that I heard what the Lord who spoke *through* me when the light of wisdom was turned on! I said, "A mother can't protect her own child; not when it is her husband (or in any other area of a child's life) since she cannot always be with them—only God can protect them! When we take the position of protection away from God, then that's when we open the child up to attacks that the Lord could have prevented if we had given it to Him."

This revelation that the Lord gave me caused me to stop to look back over my own life where I could see very clearly that when I finally gave up on protecting myself, the Lord took over and I found the safety and security that I had lacked!

Reviewing what He'd done increased my level of trust to the point that I was able to use a few years later with my children. The first time was when my husband told my children that he was divorcing me, and then later when he introduced them to the other woman he had left me for. There is nothing you or I can do to stop this kind of exposure that we, if we had the choice, would not allow our children to go through. Honestly, if you are in my position and you have divorce papers that say that your husband has these rights by law, you need to remember that even without a written document, God gave our children to both parents (to you *and* their father). So what happens when things go in a direction that we had not planned for, and fear begins to set in?

Many women today run away: sometimes for the "sake of the children" and sometimes it's for their own safety. But honestly, who of us wants to be a fugitive, to run away from their home, friends, and family, and to live constantly on the run and in fear of being found by the one we are running from? Women run because they feel that it is their only choice, but is it? Can God really be trusted to protect us if we put our trust in Him? And, sometimes, a harder question is: Can God really protect our friend or sister or my child—someone else we love when we put our trust in Him alone?

We know from scripture that David got into a bad habit of running. Though he had seen the Lord help him kill Goliath, he ran from King Saul and then years later, he ran from his own son. Most of us have been there. We run, and yet there are others who choose to stand and fight. Personally, I believe neither option protects us as women. Women long and need to be protected. So once again, can we really trust God to protect us?

Many of us have trusted Him with our eternal destiny, when we accepted Him as our Savior, but can He really save us now from what is coming against us, or coming against those whom we love and whom we want to protect? The answer is Yes, absolutely, Yes. All it takes is walking in our faith, our faith IN HIM, to see that protection materialize.

Protection, by faith, is just like any other trust: it requires us to leave it totally in God's hands. When we trust the Lord for salvation, *He* is the one who does it, not us "lest any man should boast"—we just accept it. It is nothing that we do—we just accept His free gift and believe that He has done it. We simply walk in it and trust that we are saved.

When we trust the Lord with our finances, He is the One who provides "all our needs according to His riches in Christ Jesus." If we foolishly *try* to help Him out, we find our finances are soon *not* enough to pay the bills. It takes trust. Can He be trusted?

I think to answer that question in a new area of our lives, it helps to look back at how He has protected us in other areas of our lives. If we take the time to count our blessings, and the many ways that He has protected us in the past, counting and naming them one-by-one, it helps to build our faith. This is what I have done, coupled with looking back at the times that I tried to do it myself, and failed miserably.

Let's begin with finances since this is a big area for many of you who are single mothers. When I was faced with this dilemma, with so many children living at home and no child support, God first stacked the odds against me by bringing my niece to live with us, then my older sister. You know, we should never be surprised or shocked or dismayed when things are piled on, since this is a pattern with God. It is His way of Him showing us His awesome power!!

It's then when He will step in and began to do the impossible. But it has to look impossible first. Counting and naming the times He protected me: When my finances were horribly attacked, I did not lose my home, nor did my family's standard of living drop—instead it improved!! It wasn't until I really began to get a handle on our finances, and began to try to control things, that I began to fear and our finances began to slowly diminish. It then took a turn for the better when I made the decision to not look or try to figure it out (which was so hard to do) that I discovered that my bank accounts were again full and overflowing. Can God protect us financially when we trust (and obey) Him? The answer, if you give it completely to Him is, "Yes."

Obey

You know obedience plays a big part in our protection too. So often, we are "perishing for a lack of knowledge." If we violate a scriptural principle (that is a spiritual law; like the law of gravity) over and over again, we erroneously believe that God is *not* protecting us, when in fact, it is we who have put ourselves in that place of danger.

For instance, since we were discussing finances, when we are ignorant of the command that we must tithe and if we don't we are stealing from God, we soon find ourselves in a financial mess. For those of us who have learned the blessing and the promise of tithing, and we obeyed (no matter if it looked like we couldn't afford it), and we simply trusted God—we have found Him faithful and full of favor as He surrounds us with the desires of our hearts, not just supplying our needs!! I have personally found (as so many others have told me too) that the more I trust God and give (not out of abundance, but very often when there didn't seem to be enough) that the windows of heaven opened, and showers of blessings poured over me!

No matter how much I trusted the Lord for my finances, that trust would not have resulted in abundance if I had not first known that I was told to tithe and to give (even when on paper I wouldn't have enough), and then to take the step of faith and do it. No matter how much you believe that the Lord is able to save you, it is not until you surrender your life and trust Him, that you are transformed into a new creation. It is the same way with your protection.

Finally, I had come to a place where I knew I couldn't do it: protecting myself or protecting my children. I believe that when we trust the Lord (for our children or for ourselves) that He will not always "deliver" us from the trial or crisis. God does not promise to *remove* the evil that comes against us, but He does promise to use it for our good as we walk *through* it.

Most of the time, He calls us to go *through* the fire, to spend the night *in* the lion's den, and to walk *through* the Red Sea. Though we might choose to avoid these situations, they are what ultimately makes us into new creations that show others how different we are, and how we have changed. Going through divorce (the second or third time for my older children) is what has made my children different than the rest of the crowd. It is what has given them, my children, the obvious godly character (what they are like deep-down, behind closed doors, and how they react when backed up against the wall). This godly character is what I want for my children; therefore, I am letting go, surrendering my control over their situations, and putting ALL my trust in the only One who can be trusted—my Beloved!

How can I foolishly believe that I could ever do a better job of protecting my children than I know the Lord can?

Just recently, I felt compelled to protect my special needs sister who was threatened with being put in a mental hospital by the director of her assisted living apartment. It was right in the middle of one of our women's conferences, and I just didn't have time for that trial! So as I drove to the airport, I spoke to the Lord about it, *after* trying unsuccessfully to protect my sister myself. That was when my Beloved reminded me of how, when given the opportunity (because I had turned my protection over to Him instead of protecting myself), HE protected me, and that He would do the same thing for my sister. I walked out my faith and have not tried to protect her reputation or from the examination that could (if God wasn't in control) land her in a mental hospital.

If I can't trust God, whom can I trust? All I know for certain is that He is faithful, and, what may be even better is the peace that comes from letting go and surrendering it to Him. How can we seriously opt to instead worry and/or work at something, when we know we are unable to achieve, when we could simply give it to Him rather than choosing to do it ourselves?

Many love to tell me about a situation that resulted in tragedy when a person "supposedly" trusted God. However, when I questioned them, they soon admit that the person they referred to would often take back control and try to protect themselves—don't we all? I think that is why it is usually someone else's situation that causes us not to feel safe to trust God, and this usually also causes confusion. No one really knows what goes on in another person's life, even when that person is a relative or our own children.

Don't make the mistake of looking at what you *thought* you saw in someone else's life or what you *heard*. No one but God knows their heart condition and the entire situation. Those who make their decision of faith based on a second-hand testimony are in danger of making a huge mistake, resulting in missed blessings and being vulnerable to unnecessary hardship.

Once I gave up trying to protect my reputation, that's when my reputation took a leap of prominence rather than what should have happened, considering the situation. When I gave up trying to protect my emotions, I felt the love of the Lord surrounding my heart even though so many things were coming against me: divorce, another woman, and my children participating in my spouse's wedding. In the real world, this would have devastated a wife and mother like me. However, because I trusted the Lord (and only because I trusted Him to protect my heart), I am flourishing and instead have never felt so loved!

The Lord has been working on this area of my life for quite a few years. It was probably more than two years ago when my life took a turn as I finally refused to protect myself from all kinds of abuse that happens when a husband is not happy. An unhappy husband often believes it is his wife's fault and takes it out on her. (The same is true for an unhappy woman who blames her husband). Many women with good and pure hearts try desperately to please their husbands, but the problem is often not in them to fix.

Changing myself (by following the principles with a pure heart) and protecting myself (no matter what method I tried) never worked. It wasn't until I gave up and gave it to God that He was given permission to protect me, and then He delivered me. However, I know that if I had run or continued to try on my own, I would still be afraid and searching in vain for safety and security. The blessing in living *through* that trial is that now I know that God is a God who protects— so I can trust Him with my children. Hallelujah!!

Dear reader, no matter how BIG your trial, or perpetrator, or enemy attack, God is BIGGER. He is not baffled or afraid or concerned about that thing or person who is after you. He is able to create good out of it and in every situation as long as you surrender everything to Him and trust Him for your protection (for yourself and for everyone whom you love).

Every fire refines and purifies. Every lion can shut its mouth. And every sea, no matter how large, can be quieted or divided with just one word from God.

Chapter Epilogue

Since writing this, God has already moved on behalf of my sister— let's praise Him!

First, we both let go (which includes my sister who has the faith and mind of a child) and trusted the director (who was trying to have her committed) to set up the appointment that had the potential to commit her to a mental hospital. I did not pray or fast (not because I don't believe in prayer and fasting, but because I was not "called" to fast—I simply trusted God), and the result? **The doctor told her that he did not think she needed a mental examination!!**

If that were not enough, today, my sister told me that the director, who was trying so desperately to commit her, is LEAVING. Just like that!!! She requested a transfer. WOW.

Can God be trusted? ABSOLUTELY!!

———— Chapter 13 ————

If You Love Me

If you love Me, you will keep My commandments.
—John 14:15

Thinking that this would be the final chapter of this book, I sought the Lord for the most important principle on which to conclude with: a principle that has changed my life, and that hopefully, will change your life as well.

What the Lord told me was a complete surprise. In the days since He first told me that this chapter needed to be about the *blessings of obedience* (submission and the like), He has revealed to me so much more that I hope to be able to fully share with you in this chapter. Revelation that I believe could literally change the course of your life, if that is, you take it to heart and seek to obey, no matter the cost.

The opening verse needs to be read again: *"If you love Me, you will keep My commandments" (John 14:15).*

To me, love is the key. If we love the Lord, it will show Him (and others who are watching), by how determined we are to obey Him. Now stop and think on that thought for a while.

Now, if our obedience shows our love for Him, our **lack** of obedience, or disobedience, shows Him (and others) the contrary. This means that disobedience says we do NOT love the Lord. Are you getting it?

With this principle well established for us to build upon, the Bible tells us clearly that we are each to submit to the authorities over us. If we are married, we are to submit to our husbands. If we are not married (and live at home), we are to submit to our parents. If we have parents who are still alive, we are to honor them. If we have a boss, we are to submit and be obedient to them. If we are in school, our obedience is to our teachers, our principal, etc. All of us live in a country where there are laws: traffic, public, state, local; the list of those in authority over us is endless.

The Lord tells us that for us to be blessed we MUST be obedient to each and every one of these authorities, whether or not we agree and whether or not these authorities are good and kind or even cruel. If you are still not convinced, read these two verses carefully:

"Every person is to be in subjection to the governing authorities for there is no authority except from God, and those which exist are established by God.

Therefore whoever resists authority has opposed the ordinance of God; and they who have opposed will receive condemnation upon themselves.

For rulers are not a cause of fear for good behavior, but for evil. Do you want to have no fear of authority? Do what is good and you will have praise from the same . . ." (Romans 13:1–3).

*"Servants, be submissive to your masters with all respect, not only to those who are good and gentle, but also to those who are unreasonable. For this finds favor, if for the sake of conscience toward God a person bears up under sorrows when suffering unjustly. For what credit is there if, when you sin and are harshly treated, you endure it with patience? But if when you do what is right and suffer for it you patiently endure it, this finds **favor** with God" (1 Peter 2:18–20).*

You know, when I read that last verse I understood just WHY I have been so adamant and so careful to be obedient every moment of my life. Favor. Submission finds favor with God. I do not know about you, but what I want in my life is to be surrounded by God's favor. This is how we live the abundant life—heaven on earth.

As I mentioned in the last paragraph, there is something that I really want to expound upon in this chapter and this is the reason why I said that I am "careful" to be obedient every moment of my life. Right now, I am flying home, my 17th flight (one more to go) after touring Asia, the Far East, or the Orient, as many call it. Because I have been flying extensively, I have heard and seen the safety instructions until I think that I can give the demonstration myself! However, I still pay attention and listen since I want to be in obedience to the authority of the airline, the captain, and the flight attendant. You may think this is idiotic and takes this principle of obedience too far. But if I choose to ignore this level of authority, how far will I take it—to ignore it until I walk right out of the boundary of God's favor? I am not sure how wide the boundaries of His favor are; therefore, I am very careful on every level since I don't want to risk stepping out of it.

In all the chapters I have written in this book (and the other book I have had the pleasure of writing and living through), the Lord has brought situations into my life as examples of the principles He teaches me, in order that I will share and teach them to you. Though we have really powerful women in ministry and in leadership, just recently the Lord has brought to my attention the fact that so many, so many, do not walk in obedience, and it spills over into every area of their lives. The truth is, if you are under someone's authority and you usurp that authority by doing what you want to do rather than what the person in authority asks you to do, you are in rebellion.

"For rebellion is as the sin of divination, and insubordination is as iniquity and idolatry because you have rejected the word of the LORD, He has also rejected you from being king" (1 Samuel 15:23).

Rebellion is living dangerously, and I want no part of it. As a matter of fact, I don't even want to associate with it. On this very lengthy trip, I ended up actually parting ways with a member of my women's ministry who started out traveling with me, because she was continually insubordinate. Insubordination is not the same as rebellion, although I had thought for years that it was.

Insubordination is when we take the authority that belongs to someone over us. It could be, and many times is in marriage— when a woman takes charge in their marriage and rules over her husband. In homes today, children are insubordinate almost from infancy.

Children are who are really in charge while the mother and/or father submits to their whims and demands. What a tragedy!

"O My people! Their oppressors are children, and women rule over them. O My people!" (Isaiah 3:12).

"The rod and reproof give wisdom, but a child who gets his own way brings shame to his mother" (Proverbs 29:15).

By taking authority over the one who really should be in authority over us (remember that all authority is established by God?), then we are in idolatry. Who is our idol? Ourselves. We put ourselves forth as the one to worship. Let's not forget that this is the first sin, the sin that created the demonic world that battles against us every day. Lucifer wanted to be equal or above God, and thus, sin was established. Things have never been the same since that time. Insubordination, which is idolatry, is something we must run from and avoid at all costs.

Though I would really need an entire chapter, and probably a book, to really deal with the principle of insubordination and the counterpart of honoring parents, let me just say that in the United States, we are so far off when dealing with elderly parents. Grown children today treat their parents with such little honor and respect it really makes me grieve and literally makes me sick. I will tell you that I paid a very high price to continue to honor my parents before they died: a high price. (But that needs to be another book and I am not yet ready to touch on that pain.) But I would do it again in a heartbeat if I had to go through it again. If you have grown parents, I warn you to be very careful how you speak to them, speak about them, and how you treat them.

"Honor your father and your mother, as the LORD your God has commanded you, that your days may be prolonged and that it may go well with you on the land which the LORD your God gives you" (Deuteronomy 5:16).

*"For God said, 'HONOR YOUR FATHER AND MOTHER,' and, 'HE WHO **SPEAKS** EVIL OF FATHER OR MOTHER IS TO BE PUT TO DEATH'" (Matthew 15:4).*

And let me say that there is no excuse for treating your parents as if they were *your* child; not even when they are plagued with dementia (such as Alzheimer's). You can still honor what you *know* they would want, just like women who begin to submit to their husbands who are gone. Honor them by making decisions for them since you know what they would want if they could express it to you. And don't make the excuse that your decision is for their good when that's just an excuse to hide behind, because God sees your heart.

The wisdom and understanding I'm sharing with you came by going through it when I did it all wrong, and then finding the path to righteousness as I sought the Lord. When my father was hospitalized, he was told that he needed a pacemaker. He very kindly told the doctors (and his family) that he had lived a long life and that that he didn't want one. Unfortunately, I had his "power of attorney," and with that power, I was a target for my siblings (I am one of eleven children) to push me to make the decision against my father's wishes "since he obviously couldn't choose for himself" they all agreed, but this was well before dementia ever hit him. I regrettably signed the papers for him to get the pacemaker.

For the next few years, I watched my father die a slow death to the point that he spent the last nine months of his life bedridden. My siblings didn't witness his suffering since they lived states away and some in other countries. So due to what I'd done, I watched my hero (who was once a famous and talented artist) not be able to sign his name or feed himself. To date it had been the biggest mistake of my life when I signed the papers for that pacemaker and dishonored my father. I paid a high price for my insubordination.

Yet as we all know, God is a God of second chances. Within five years, I had my chance to redeem myself and to learn a very hard lesson about honoring a parent, no matter the cost. First, I had to repent to my mother regarding dishonoring my father. She, too, had to suffer and care for him and to watch him die slowly, painfully and with horrible humiliation. Though God did use that time for good (Romans 8:28) because my mother helped as one of the editors of *A Wise Woman* book, working with me when Erin revised it. And although she said that the principles were for other women, not for her, God changed her. Then He gave her another chance to be the wife that I know she had probably always wanted to be for my father. She was able to redeem what the locusts had eaten. God is awesome. Thank you Erin.

Let me now continue to share about my second chance. It came in the year 2000, five years after my dad died. My mom became weak and sickly but she did not want to go to the doctor. She had always been like that. As a matter of fact, after my father died, while I was taking care of all the insurance paperwork, the insurance company asked when my mother had died. I told the lady that she didn't; she was still living. The reason she believed she'd died was that her insurance records showed that the last time she had seen a doctor was in 1959, which was the day my youngest sister was born—a full thirty-nine years without seeing a doctor.

So as my mother became more ill, just as before, I began to receive a lot of pressure from my siblings, insisting that I had to get my mother to a doctor—I refused. Within weeks, my mother began to speak to me about "*when* I die . . ." She told me honestly and very calmly that either Jesus would heal her or she would go to heaven. No doctor.

No matter what it cost me, I was determined to honor my mother and to obey. Just a few short weeks later, while I was cleaning her room, my mother died in her own bed, no doctor. I stood there listening, but she didn't take another breath. Calmly, I called the funeral home. (My mother and I had made prior arrangements together when we had gone there for my father's arrangements.) They told me that since she died at home, I needed to call paramedics to confirm her death. When they arrived, the police came as well, and within a few minutes, I had five different officers asking me questions. It was the last plainclothes policeman who asked me, "Do you have any idea what is happening?" When I said "no," he told me very kindly that I was being charged with the death of my mother. Since I had not sought medical help, and as I was with her during her death and did not call 911 when I knew she was dying, I was being charged with taking her life.

As I said, this really needs to be another book, but as you have probably guessed, the charges were *eventually* dropped after many lengthy investigations. But the criminal charges were later followed by Family Services charging me with "abuse, neglect, and exploitation of an elderly person." These charges were also dropped, many months later, and after many lengthy investigations. It also kept me from attending my mother's memorial service and it requiring special permission from the state to be allowed to move out of state with my family.

Needless to say, it was a nightmare that few will ever face. I had paid a high price to honor and obey my mother's wishes, but as I have said before, if I had it to do again, I would gladly pay the price.

One thing that I do know for certain is that I have shown honor as a daughter to my parents. Therefore, I am assured that my children will honor me and I am seeing it already. Throughout my married life, I witnessed first-hand my former husband dishonoring his parents. Without really understanding the grave consequences, he and his older brother are notorious for trying to tell, especially their mother, what to do and not do. There were many loud, public disputes and disagreements, very often about how she spent her time and money. I was never really in the position to be able to talk to my former husband about it when we were married (since this would be the same insubordination as I am sharing about here). After we were divorced, however, I was able to talk to him briefly about my concern.

Currently, my former husband is living with his mother. Though we don't really talk now (since he is presently engaged; we are friendly but no longer friends like we were), he told me how horrible it was to have her treat him as a kid. How she got on him about everything, especially his drinking. I thought to myself that maybe God was giving him a second chance to get things right with his mother. I am not sure if he knows it, nor if he will take the opportunity to honor his mother, but the consequences may be more than he bargained for. Though my children are very, very respectful of all authority, I was in utter shock and surprise that my children have never encouraged me to seek restoration with their father. As a matter of fact, they're against it. When he moved states away, and later planned to move back to the area where we live "if he had the money," it was my children who did not want me to give him the money. Insubordination is sin and the Bible is clear, what we sow, we will indeed reap.

As I said, this is not the way my children usually are. They have *never* been disrespectful to him, spoken against him, or refused to see or speak to him. All I can say is that this verse is also true:

"Do not be deceived, God is not mocked; for whatever a man sows, this he will also reap" (Galatians 6:7).

Now that we've covered insubordination, what exactly then does it mean to be obedient? Sometimes, we need to see what *not* being obedient is to fully understand what obedience is. Here is an example of disobedience from one of our television members that I observed just last night. I was invited to stay overnight with this member (when she heard I was traveling to this area), who interestingly was separated from her husband. But then, at the last minute, this woman's husband told her that he was not comfortable with me staying in their home. However, it was going to create a big expense for me with last-minute arrangements, so she told me that I could still stay at her home since her husband had left early in the morning and he wouldn't know. I was more than shocked, but I realized she honestly had no idea that what she did was disobedience or rebellion. This woman loves the Lord but she had no idea that she was doing anything wrong.

During this same week, one of the ladies who works for RMI as a volunteer had one incident after another of disobedience, coupled with insubordination when she made decisions without checking with Erin (since Erin had given her instructions, but she chose to do something else). When I saw what had happened, I spent a lot of time and tried my best to explain how to obey, what constituted disobedience, and how insubordination played into the scheme of things that would go very wrong. In one email, this woman stated that she did not **"try** to be rebellious," to which the Lord told me "you don't have to *try* to be rebellious, it comes naturally; you have to *try* to be obedient." Wow.

I believe that the root of rebellion, disobedience, and even insubordination, goes all the way back to our relationship with the

Lord. How many times have we known what we should do but we have chosen to do something else? How many times have we excused, ignored, or reasoned why we did something that someone in authority told us not to do or what we were to do but we chose not to do it?

As I mentioned earlier, I am on my way back home after many, many, many flights. I still hate flying. I still hate being away from family. But though I hate flying (but thankfully have no fear of flying like Erin's shared that she has), I love the Lord so much more and it shows by obeying Him. Before I even got home, my church had already booked an extensive tour to Africa and Europe that may even include time in South America. Many of you who love to travel may envy me, but those who are closest to me see clearly that I love the Lord with all my heart, because they all know that I hate to travel and I am a simple homebody. I've always been happiest at home and am very content to just care for my home and family. So if given a choice, I would remain home. However, I love the Lord, and it shows through my obedience to Him.

"If you love Me . . ." *(John 14:15).*

What about you? At what level of obedience do you live? Trust me, for most of you, you have no idea that you are living in rebellion, disobedience, or insubordination. I have just witnessed this phenomenon with three of our church members whom I know love the Lord and are passionate in their desire to gain a greater intimacy with Him. But, if these sins (rebellion, disobedience, or insubordination) are active in your life, then deep intimacy with the Lord is simply impossible. This is not my opinion but God's. And the only way that you can break this cycle, which stands in the way of true intimacy with Him, is to first admit that you are a sinner.

"If we say that we have no sin, we are deceiving ourselves and the truth is not in us" (1 John 1:8).

Secondly, ask the Lord to reveal the areas where you are living in rebellion. He will.

Finally, begin to watch your day-to-day living habits to see ways to obey. Remember we don't need to try to disobey, we need to try to obey. Then, once you begin this enhanced journey, you will be amazed how great it is to walk in God's perfect will where you are always surrounded with favor and blessings. One of my greatest benefits is watching my own children who are "walking in the truth" as fruits of my obedience and now I can share John's sentiments: "I have no greater joy than this" (3 John 1:4).

Chapter 14

You're All that Matters

One thing I have asked from the LORD, that I shall seek:
That I may dwell in the house of the LORD
all the days of my life,
To behold the beauty of the LORD
And to meditate in His temple.
—Psalm 27:4

In seeking the Lord for what to write in this final chapter, there were many principles I could have shared. Oh, how fitting that I would end up concluding with what matters in my life—Him and Him alone! Just ***One thing*** *I have asked from the LORD . . .*

Due to facing an onslaught of crises in my life, very often throughout the day I am surprised and yet increasingly filled with awe that instead of fear or panic or planning an escape, I instead feel this overwhelming passion for Him. So I inevitably ask the Lord to help me to *somehow* have the words to explain the total blessedness, sheer joy and incredible awesomeness of knowing Him from the moment I took Him as my Husband, since no one seems to really understand. Yet that's to be expected, since I, too, had no clue whatsoever prior to my living it.

Very often, especially lately, I stop to ponder how I used to think and feel about things. For instance, with my former husband's wedding date just days away, I remember how I used to envy women who had godly husbands. You know, the same sort of woman who I know looked at me, since I once had a pastor for a husband before he walked away. So many women, I know, before everything in my life became public, told me they'd sit in their pew looking at me, longingly, while they'd be sitting next to their husband who wasn't interested in spiritual matters or things pertaining to Him. Looks, dear one, can be deceiving. Yet I actually did the very same thing, so I assume that's why I got what I coveted. Thankfully, He's so loving that He brings us through those valleys and still sees fit to bless us in spite of ourselves.

So, first let me say something I know you already know by now—don't go by what you think you see. Many of those women whom you envy are in far worse shape than you are in. Like me, they have husbands who appear spiritual, are outwardly a spiritual giant, so other women envy us, and often say so publically, when in truth the man and our dream life is not as you imagine it to be. And because of the way you misunderstand her, she has compounded pain when she chooses to honor her "less than honorable" husband. We each must admit that no one knows what really goes on behind closed doors after a man (or woman) leaves the pulpit or after leading worship, or in the lives of those whom you watch on television. I know.

Yet, of course there are women who are blessed with incredible husbands, some who have even changed history. So I used to envy these women too. But now I know that if any woman knew the life that I lead right now, they would instead envy me! And what thrills me beyond belief and the totally unimaginable truth is that this life can be the same for each and every one of you! I am not the only bride whom He has called. Each and every of you has the very same opportunity to become His bride—no matter what your marital status, social status, physical stature, spiritual state, or mental capabilities. It makes me tear up knowing that He loves you just as you are and loves you, not in spite of, but because of your weaknesses! "While we were yet sinners, Christ died for us"—Awesome; simply awesome!

When I used to work with Erin, back when her ministry was more of a "marriage restoration" ministry, she and I knew there was no guarantee that the woman who came looking for help would be able to follow the principles (to the letter) in order obtain a restored marriage. And worse, once it was restored, there were varying degrees of blessedness depending on the man who returned home. But now, this has all changed! The new call on my life and Erin's focus has begun to focus on recruiting brides for our Beloved. Everyone (even men though it's harder to wrap my head around) are called to be the bride for whom He is coming back for *"that He might present to Himself the church in all her glory, having no **spot** or **wrinkle** or any such thing; but that she would be holy and blameless" (Ephesians 5:27).* This means, each and every woman can simply trust Him, seek Him only, and everyone who desires to be loved and healed and happy can be! Nevertheless, this only happens when you and I are willing to let go and lose the life we had planned on. This is because He needs our whole heart to be free to then have it all.

*"For whoever wishes to save his **life** will **lose** it; but whoever **loses** his **life** for My sake will **find** it" (Matthew 16:25).*

"The woman who is unmarried, and the virgin, is concerned about the things of the Lord, that she may be holy both in body and spirit; but one who is married is concerned about the things of the world, how she may please her husband" (1 Corinthians 7:34).

*"An unmarried woman or virgin is concerned about the Lord's affairs: Her aim is to be devoted to the Lord in both body and spirit. But **a married woman is concerned about the affairs of this world— how she can please her husband.** I am saying this for your own good, not to restrict you, but that you may live in a right way **in undivided devotion to the Lord"** (1 Corinthians 7:34).*

*"Delight yourself in the LORD; and He will give you the **desires** of your **heart"** (Psalms 37:4).*

When my life bottomed out about a year ago (with my husband divorcing me to marry someone else), it was the end of the life I had hoped and dreamed for most of my life. Yet, by losing my preplanned life, and opening my heart, I opened amazingly new and exciting experiences that changed my world. It's my hope that you will have the courage to do the same and what I've shared will help change your life in the very same way.

One amazing truth that I learned is that He never meant that we had to literally *die* to live in paradise, nor do we have to wait until He comes to get us as His bride. *"Let us rejoice and be glad and give the glory to Him, for the marriage of the Lamb has come and **His bride** has made herself ready" (Revelations19:7).* Let's be real, there are far too many women who are hurting horribly: abandoned, forsaken and grieved to think that this is the way we women were supposed to live until we die. The way we've been taught to believe is simply not correct!

Jesus didn't die so we could, one day, go to heaven. He laid His life down to set us free now, in every area of our lives; His blood and His resurrection changed it all and it was for now. This means that women who are ignorant to this truth will continue to perish in their lack of knowledge and hope. *"My people are destroyed for lack of knowledge. Because you have rejected knowledge . . ." (Hosea 4:6).* Unless we live our lives in such a way as to reflect what they too can have, and when asked we simply share our hearts that are overflowing with love!

He Is Making All Things New!

This morning, I guess you could say that I came to the end of myself, or maybe it's simply facing the end of my ministry as it was, or maybe it's both. However, I am far from concerned, afraid, or any other negative emotion. I am simply excited to see what is about to happen. This morning when I woke up, and spoke to the Lord about it, He gave me a new revelation or principle. He told me that **it takes us thanking Him, and *being broken*, in order for us to be blessed.**

*". . . and He took the seven loaves and the fish; and **giving thanks, He broke them** and started giving them to the disciples, and the disciples gave them to the people" (Matthew 15:36).*

*"And He directed the people to sit down on the ground; and taking the seven loaves, **He gave thanks and broke them,** and started giving them to His disciples to serve to them, and they served them to the people" (Mark 8:6).*

*"And when He had taken some bread and **given thanks,** He **broke it** and gave it to them, saying, 'This is My body which is given for you; do this in remembrance of Me'" (Luke 22:19).*

*"Having said this, he took bread and **gave thanks to God** in the presence of all, and **he broke it** and began to eat" (Acts 27:35).*

*". . . and **when He had given thanks, He broke it** and said, 'This is My body, which is for you; do this in remembrance of Me'" (1 Corinthians 11:24).*

The only way to multiply, and the only way for His glory to appear, is when we give thanks and allow ourselves to be *broken* in order to feed those who are hungry for the truth, in order to heal those who are unloved.

This morning, I had to face the fact that the way things LOOK is that my ministry within the church is going under. But we all know (or should know by now) that it is always darkest before the dawn; that to have a resurrection, there has to be a death; that without an enemy cornering you, there is no Red Sea to part. To encourage me further, the Lord had me read through the promises He had given me in Isaiah and Jeremiah, all the way through to Malachi. I cried buckets of tears (of joy) when I saw that 90 percent of those promises have already been fulfilled. Therefore, these new crises are simply what will catapult me to experience the fulfillment of the final 10 percent of the remaining promises, which often mean it's when we will face our greatest trials. This is the reason why the Apostle Paul spoke so often to encourage his readers not to faint and to finish the race.

No matter how things look, I want to let go and let everything be allowed to fail and to fall. Just as I have done in the past, I just give it all up and simply surrender it to the Lord. I told Him that it really doesn't matter anyway, because He is all that I want and need, so I care little to nothing if I lose it all (even though my church ministry is my family's only income, which means that the loss of my ministry means our home would be gone also)—dear Lord, you're all that matters to me!

It's also not just about me. My children are all watching and waiting, and at the same time, they are looking (and commenting often) because their dad is who is currently prospering, while more and more of what I have or had is crumbling. Yet they know, and we remind each other that righteousness will, always and forever, play out in the end. This is the way God created the universe, so it is foolish for us to become anxious about what's ahead, isn't it?

"Thus says the LORD, 'Cursed is the man who trusts in mankind and makes flesh his strength, and whose heart turns away from the LORD. For he will be like a bush in the desert and will not see when prosperity comes, but will live in stony wastes in the wilderness, a land of salt without inhabitant'" (Jeremiah 17:5–6).

The Plot Thickens

Interestingly, my church ministry "apparently" crumbling is not the half of it, for what I am about to share will shake most of you. It's been exactly two weeks ago today that I got an email from my FH that rocked my world. It was my "Abraham-Isaac-altar heart test." It is only because of Him and His love for me that helped me to go through it with joy and without any trace of fear. I am amazed at how He has changed and transformed "Much-Afraid," yep, that's me!

The email came on what *would have been* my 25th wedding anniversary, which forced me to face a couple of things that I knew I could possibly (no, I guess I knew it would be a probability) be facing in the future. The attack was two-fold.

First, my FH explained he was taking custody of my three youngest children when he married, which is now less than two weeks from today. Aren't you glad that *"We are hard pressed on every side, but not crushed; perplexed, but not in despair; persecuted, but not abandoned; struck down, but not destroyed" (2 Corinthians 4:8–9)*?

I knew, without any doubt or fear, that *whatever* was about to happen would be a good thing. It could mean that I may live hours away from my children, but if so, then it would be a good thing. How that would be possible, I don't have a clue; but no one could have convinced me a year ago that I could have experienced such JOY by having a husband walk out, tell me he was going to look for someone else to marry, divorce me, leave me with all our debt, not pay child support, have a judgment that would ruin my credit for ten years, and set out to destroy my resources (our family's livelihood) while away ministering in Hong Kong, *and* that my children would be in my FH wedding party when he marry the AW.

**Forgive me for sharing these details with you, but I did so to remind me, too, of the sheer awesomeness of God!! How often we fail to really ponder and think of all that He has done for us!!

So with the same enthusiasm as I exhibited with the divorce that turned to joy instead of sorrow, I embraced the crisis, and in a matter of just 48 hours, the tide had turned so incredibly that all I could do was praise the Lord and fall in love with Him all over again! This crisis took place in order to bless my children and me. Though it might have been intended for evil, God intended it for good. In the end, instead of my youngest children moving away to live with their father and the AW, it caused things to be uncovered in their little hearts, which resulted in my FH making plans to come here to visit them (and without the AW) at least for now!

This crisis inevitably uncovered the truth that, the hurried nature of my FH's decision to move out, divorce me, move away, and the most traumatic event of them being introduced to the AW and having her in their lives, had resulted in our children pulling away from loving their dad because the pain had become too great for them to bear. Had I tried to stop or slow down anything my FH wanted to do this year, I would not (and my children would not) be experiencing the newfound freedom and joy we are now rejoicing in!! Even the once "very exciting wedding" is now a very bittersweet event since for him. This is, once again, subjecting the children to what could potentially destroy the love entirely, the love they once had for their father. My FH knows it and has expressed it, yet he also knows he can't stop the children from coming and witnessing an event that could alter their future relationship with him forever.

The second attack in my FH's email made it *very* clear that destroying our resources was not enough—they (he and his fiancée) are determined to stop my church ministry completely, stating many lies and slander. They've made it clear they want me out of the "marriage ministry" for good, both at our church and my association with RMI. And my FH said that whatever it takes he will take his children away from me. However, *"'No weapon that is formed against you will prosper; and every tongue that accuses you in judgment you will condemn, this is the heritage of the servants of the LORD, and their vindication is from Me," declares the LORD"* (Isaiah 54:17). Knowing His truth meant when I heard the threats, I was not moved at all, instead, I became more excited to see what blessings would result from this frontal attack.

So, not only did I place my children on the altar of my heart, I also went ahead and officially placed my church ministry and my volunteering with RMI, along with my potential future of being entirely alone, giving everything to the Lord because all of it is His anyway!

Immediately, the Lord spoke to me ever so gently in my prayer closet concerning what I had to do. Honestly, though, it was something that He put on my heart a very long time ago; back when my ex-husband* was still running the ministry. The Lord told me to let go of everything and resign from each of my positions.

My FH told me that I cannot use those initials for him anymore; therefore, you will see that I will begin referring to him as my ex or ex-husband, not FH.

Though I no longer "submit" to my ex-husband since he is no longer my husband, we are told not to resist evil and to do more than is asked of us. "But I say to you, do not resist an evil person; but whoever slaps you on your right cheek, turn the other to him also. If anyone wants to sue you and take your shirt, let him have your coat also. Whoever forces you to go one mile, go with him two. Give to him who asks of you, and do not turn away from him who wants to borrow from you" (Matthew 5:40–42).

*This principle is very different than **submitting** to a husband, and needs the leading of the Holy Spirit to really walk it out since there is no easy way of discerning.*

So, by letting go, I believe I will have more time to write and for now, spend time with my children!! I'm not sure where our income will come from, but it's God who provides for *"all of our needs according to His riches"* so why should you or I worry?

God truly is in control, so that should make ALL OF US just rest in Him, no longer worried that we will make a mistake or miss God. It's only when we are surrounded by the enemy and getting backed up to that huge Red Sea, that God parts it! And once parted it creates a clean, straight path directing us to EXACTLY where He wants us to go!!

Whether I have an outlet to minister, have children close to me to love, I nevertheless will happily continue to focus on my intimacy and oneness with the Lord. Finding my Love, at last, is what I share when I meet with any woman, here where I live and women around the world. If He opens the doors for me to continue to speak in churches and conferences my message will forever be **"He is all that matters."**

Dear reader, it is all about Him becoming our Husband and us becoming His bride. And this happens only when we are willing to embrace *enthusiastically whatever* He allows to come against us— that's when the crises will result in "no more tears and no more sorrow." No threat of losing my children or ministry or income or home can shake me, because all I want and need is Him. And though people may think I am being taken advantage of, just like Jesus, no one takes my life, I lay it down willingly.

Just as Erin has been quoted as saying too, *"My beloved is mine, and I am His . . . When I found Him whom my soul loves; I held on to Him and would not let him go . . . For I am [indeed] lovesick" (Song of Solomon 3:2–4; 5:8).* May you each become lovesick too.

About the Author

Michele Michaels came to Restore Ministries International when she was facing divorce. At the time she was the mother of two small boys. After reading *How God Can and Will Restore Your Marriage* and *A Wise Woman* and she began helping Erin Thiele with her books, soon after they met while each was in Orlando, Florida. Very soon after Erin visited Michele in her home in Colorado, her marriage was restored.

Almost exactly fourteen years later Michele found herself facing divorce again while helping to update and revise a small Facing Divorce booklet for her church. After returning to RMI to Refresh her mind, Michele began to realize He had planned to use this trial for much good. It was during this new chapter in her life when Michele discovered the real reason God allowed another divorce to happen again and what she had been missing: The Abundant Life.

Michele's book *Living the Abundant Life* is available on **EncouragingBookstore.com** and also on **Amazon.com**.

Also, if you've found the freedom to love and be loved by your Husband by reading this book, make sure you read Michele's next book *Breaking free from* ***The Poverty Mentality*** and ***Moving Mountains*** available soon from these same booksellers.

Also Available

Our Abundant Life Series

on EncouragingBookstore.com & Amazon.com

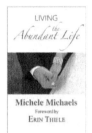 Living the Abundant Life

 Breaking Free from the Poverty Mentality

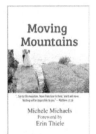 Moving Mountains

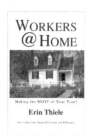 Workers @ Home: Making the MOST of Your Time!

 Home Schooling for Him: Enter by the Narrow Gate

Please visit our Websites where you'll also find these books as FREE Courses for women.

Our Restore Series

on EncouragingBookstore.com & Amazon.com

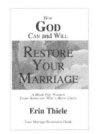

How God Can and Will Restore Your
Marriage: From Someone Who's Been There

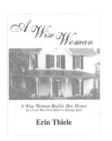

A Wise Woman: A Wise Woman Builds Her
House By a FOOL Who First Built on Sinking
Sand

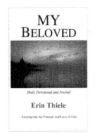

My Beloved: Daily Devotional and Journal
Coming into the Presence and Love of God

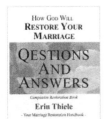

How God Will Restore Your Marriage:
Questions and Answers

 What to Do When Facing Divorce

 Facing Divorce, Again: Enthusiastically and without Fear

Please visit our Websites where you'll also find these books as FREE Courses for women.

By the Word of Their Testimony Series

on EncouragingBookstore.com & Amazon.com

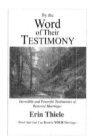
By the Word of Their Testimony: Incredible and Powerful Testimonies of Restored Marriages

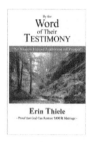
By the Word of Their Testimony: "No Weapon Formed Against you will Prosper"

By the Word of Their Testimony: "Nothing is Impossible with God"

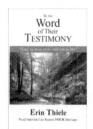
By the Word of Their Testimony: "Take up your cross and follow Me"

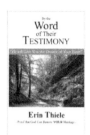

By the Word of Their Testimony: "He Will Give you the Desires of Your Heart"

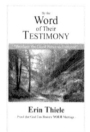

By the Word of Their Testimony: "Proclaim the Good News to Everyone"

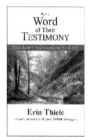

By the Word of Their Testimony: "Proclaim the Good News to Everyone"

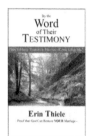

Word of Their Testimony (Book 8): You will have Treasure in Heaven —Come, follow Me

Books for Men
on EncouragingBookstore.com & Amazon.com

How God Will Restore Your Marriage: There's Healing After Broken Vows: A Book for Men

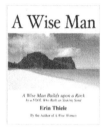

A Wise Man: A Wise Man Builds upon a Rock by a Fool Who Built on Sinking Sand

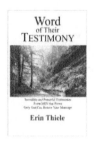

Word of Their Testimony: Incredible and Powerful Testimonies From MEN that Prove Only God Can Restore Your Marriage

Please visit our Websites where you'll also find these books as FREE Courses for both men and women:

Restore Ministries International
POB 830 Ozark, MO 65721

For more help
Please visit one of our Websites:

EncouragingWomen.org

HopeAtLast.com

RestoreMinistries.net

RMIEW.com

RMIOU.com

Aidemaritale.com (French)

AjudaMatrimonial.com (Portuguese)

AyudaMatrimonial.com (Spanish)

Pag-asa.org (Tagalog Filipino)

UiteindelikHoop.com (Afrikaans)

ZachranaManzelstva.com (Slovak)

EncouragingMen.org